Reading and Rhetoric

Edited by ROBERT B. KAPLAN
UNIVERSITY OF SOUTHERN CALIFORNIA

Reading and Rhetoric

THE ODYSSEY PRESS · INC · *New York*

PRINTED IN THE UNITED STATES

Library of Congress Catalog Card Number: 63-22604

A 098765432

INTRODUCTION

TO THE TEACHER

There are already a great many readers on the market, and it hardly seems necessary to add to the abundance with one more effort. This reader is designed for a particular purpose which, it seems to me, is not satisfied by any other work presently available. Great numbers of students come to the United States each year to study everything from anthropology to zoology, and many of these students are handicapped in their pursuit of higher education by their deficiencies in English. More and more universities and colleges are beginning to recognize the need for more intensified English training and are attempting to meet it with special courses in English as a Second Language. Of course, textbooks have been prepared for such purposes. But it seems to me that many of the textbooks in this field suffer from one of two distinct disadvantages: either they are composed of materials which, because of their simplicity and condescension insult the often highly developed intelligence and mature sophistication of the international student; or they are composed of materials which, mistakenly, strive to give the international student a very contemporary view of American life, and which as a result present that student with selections containing cultural assumptions far beyond his grasp.

This textbook attempts to do two things. First, it tries to avoid the sins of which I have accused other texts. Second, it tries to present its materials according to a rhetorical pattern, so that it may conveniently be synchronized with a writing and grammar course. Each selection is supplied with exercises intended to increase the student's vocabulary, to stimulate his interest in structure as well as in content, and to provide him with topics and models for his own writing. At the same time, the selections are chosen with an eye to introducing the student to some of the basic cultural assumptions and simple facts of American civilization. Generally, the writers selected represent the best achievements in English expository style. Certain other authors are included for examples of type or for content.

It might possibly be objected that I have tampered with the originals. All but the two final selections have been carefully edited to provide a vocabulary that the average international student can be expected to comprehend, and to employ a syntax which avoids some of the more obscure, archaic, or involved English constructions. In each case I have tried to retain as much of the original as possible. In a very few instances I am afraid that certain characteristics of style have had to be sacrificed in the interests of readability.

Very little fiction has been included. Fiction is one of the most sophisticated literary forms, and students who have difficulty in reading a language should not be exposed first to its most difficult forms. After the student has mastered the mechanics of the language and grasped some of the basic cultural assumptions, then he will be prepared to pursue his reading not only into fiction, but into poetry as well. But in the classroom he will be reading expository prose for the most part. While it may not be the highest literary form, it is at least the most functional, the most common, and the easiest to learn.

The selections in this collection are necessarily brief. The reasons for brevity are twofold. First, the shorter selections isolate particular rhetorical problems out of much longer works. Second, shorter selections are easier for the beginning and intermediate student to absorb. The student simply may not have time to overcome the greater range of difficulties present in very long selections. The briefer selection, with close attention paid to every aspect of its structure in the classroom, provides a better learning tool for the neophyte. On the other hand, in textbooks designed for American students there is a perfectly valid objection to the use of "snippets." Students who already read the language fluently are trying to learn elements of style far beyond the limitations of the beginning international student and therefore should be exposed to complete works.

While this book attempts to treat realistically the problems of the international student, it scrupulously avoids both condescension and the establishing of a double standard. The international student is not an American student in a freshman composition course, and the teacher must not lose sight of the difference. He must always remember the gulf between the intellectual sophistication of the international student and his linguistic inexperience.

It is perfectly apparent that this text is in no sense definitive. It is intended only to fill a present need. These selections have worked well in my own classes, and I believe that they will serve others equally well. These readings seem to me to satisfy the immediate needs of the international student by providing him with content, vocabulary, rhetoric, and basic culture, without either offending his intelligence or ignoring his deficiencies.

TO THE STUDENT

This reader is designed to introduce you to the reading of literary English. Each of the writers represented here is reasonably well known and has been selected because of his good expository style.

To introduce you to the various types of expository writing, the selections have been divided into groups representing various rhetorical structures. These divisions are admittedly somewhat artificial, because in actual practice, it is almost impossible to find pure examples of the various types. Except in a dictionary, for example, definition is almost never found in an isolated situation. Instead it is often used in the context of other writing to illustrate or clarify certain points. Still, it is profitable to study the types so that when you find an opportunity to use them in various combinations you will know what to do and how to do it. It is much like the study of medicine. The organs of the human body are studied in isolation, although normally they never function separately. But the medical student must understand the individual structure and function of each part in order to understand the function and structure of the whole body. Similarly, the student of language studies the rhetorical types in order to understand the body of language as a whole.

Understanding, then, that the divisions of this book are in a sense artificial, and understanding that any study is the application of an intellectual discipline, you should profit from the study of this book. If you diligently read the selections and do the exercises, you will increase your vocabulary, you will come to understand the basic structure of the English language, and you will learn various traits of western culture.

You will notice that certain words and phrases in the selections have been italicized. They may be unfamiliar to you as vocabulary, or they may serve special grammatical and rhetorical functions which you should learn. The exercises consequently focus special attention on these terms.

No single reader will solve all of your language problems, but if you wish to learn, this book can help you. If you use it as it is designed to be used, you will be able to improve your knowledge of English in all of its manifestations.

Contents

Reading and Rhetoric

SECTION I

Description

SAMUEL LANGHORNE CLEMENS

My Home Town

When I was a boy, I lived in a small city located on the bank of the Mississippi River. I can picture that old time to myself now, just as it was then. The little white town *drowsed* in the sunshine of a summer's morning. The streets were empty, or nearly so. One or two clerks were sitting in front of the Main Street stores, with their chairs tilted back against the walls, chins on breasts, hats *slouched* over their faces, asleep. A sow and a litter of pigs loafed along the sidewalk, eating watermelon rinds and seeds. Two or three lonely little freight piles were scattered about the *levee.* There was a pile of *skids* on the slope of the stone-paved *wharf,* and the *fragrant* town drunk was asleep in the shade of them. No one was there to listen to the peaceful *lapping* of the *waves* against the wharf. Then there was the great Mississippi, the majestic, the magnificent Mississippi, rolling its mile-wide tide along, shining in the sun. And the dense forest away on the other side, the point of land above the town, and the point below *bounded* the riverview and turned it into a sort of sea; a very still and brilliant and lonely one. Presently a film of dark smoke appeared above one of these *remote* points, and the steamboat appeared on the distant *horizon.*

From *Life on the Mississippi* (1883).

Exercises and Questions for Analysis

I

Define each of the following italicized words as used in the context of the sentence:

1. The little white town *drowsed* in the sunshine . . .
2. Their hats were *slouched* over their faces.
3. Freight piles were scattered about the *levee.*
4. There was a pile of *skids* on the *wharf.*
5. The *fragrant* town drunk was asleep.
6. The *waves lapped* against the wharf.
7. The dense forest and the points above and below the town *bounded* the river-view.
8. Smoke appeared above one of these *remote* points.
9. The steamboat appeared on the distant *horizon.*

II

Answer the following questions:

1. Notice that this selection takes place in the past. The author says in his first sentence, "When I was a boy, I lived . . ." But, Clemens' statement is not really necessary because the verb endings signal the time. Notice the *ed* endings. Change each of the verbs in sentences four through ten to the present tense—to the future tense. What is the effect of these changes on the selection?
2. The nouns in the fifth sentence are plural. How do you know? Make this sentence singular.
3. *Fragrant, remote,* and *distant* can also have noun and adverb forms. What are these forms? What endings are used to form these nouns?
4. Why don't native speakers of English ever say "the white little town," or "the red big schoolhouse"? What principle of word order is involved?

III

Reading is a creative process, for a selection should inspire thought, imitation, and recreation. Read the following statements closely and be sure that you understand them. Then answer the questions and write the assignments:

1. This selection is obviously descriptive. How does it differ from other descriptions which you might have read before? What is the basic purpose of description? In what ways does it succeed or fail?

2. Notice that the whole picture is presented in a particular way. The reader is first given an overall view of the town. Then the reader is led through the main street of the town, down to the river. Finally, the still picture is resolved into action by the arrival of the steamboat. This technique is very much like the technique used in many movies. What advantages or disadvantages do you find in this method?

3. Notice that there are five specific details used to describe the town itself (the clerks, the pigs, the freight piles, the drunk, and the skids). Why are these particular details chosen in preference to others? The writer might have also used any number of other details. Since he mentions the stores along the main street, for example, he might well have described the goods displayed in the store windows. But he did not choose to do so. He obviously selected and arranged these details with conscious care. What was his purpose?

4. Write a description of your own home town. You need not imitate the method employed by Clemens; in fact, it would be better if you did not. But try to use enough detail to give the reader a sense of the flavor of your home town.

HUDSON STRODE

The Market at Toluca

The road leading into Toluca becomes thickly dotted with Indians. Some ride on *burros;* some lead burros laden with produce in baskets. Some drive goats and turkeys before them. Some bear sacks on their backs or trays on their heads. Women, wrapped about the head with pigeon-blue *scarves,* bear babies on their backs, hold *toddlers* by one hand while they use the other to carry *foodstuffs* or some *handicraft* work.

The narrow streets and lanes leading into the market are crammed with Indians, their dark skins glistening like copper or bronze in the bright sun, their *varicolored cloaks* looking like a mass of *palette* colors smeared together. In the open plaza outside the market the crowd mills about. A kind of *blending* of Indian talk in various *dialects* creates a strange *droning* noise. A jackass *brays;* a turkey cock *gobbles;* a dog *yelps;* a church bell clangs. On the narrow sidewalks, merchandise is spread so *haphazardly* that in order to pass, pedestrians have to press against the wall or leap the displays. Wrinkled old women *squat* over charcoal *braziers* cooking *corn cakes,* or black beans, or pink coconut candy. Mothers sit on the curb nursing their babies. There is the smell of animal dung mingled with the odor of *carnations* and *heliotrope* from the flower *stalls.*

Exercises and Questions for Analysis

I

Define each of the following italicized words as used in the context of the sentence:

1. Some ride on *burros.*
2. Women wrap their heads in pigeon-blue *scarves.*
3. Women hold *toddlers* by the hand.
4. They carry *foodstuffs* or *handicraft* work.
5. Their *varicolored cloaks* look like a mass of *palette* colors smeared together.
6. A kind of *blending* of Indian talk in various *dialects* creates a strange *droning* noise.
7. A jackass *brays;* a turkey cock *gobbles;* a dog *yelps.*
8. Merchandise is spread so *haphazardly* that pedestrians have to press against the walls.
9. Old women *squat* over charcoal *braziers* cooking *corn cakes.*
10. There is the smell of animal dung mingled with the odor of *carnations* and *heliotrope* from the flower *stalls.*

II

Answer the following questions:

1. What tense is employed in this selection? What is the effect of using this tense? What would happen if the past tense were used? Change the first ten sentences to the past tense.
2. In the sentence, "A jackass brays; a turkey cock gobbles; a dog yelps; a church bell clangs," all the verbs end with an "*s.*" Why? What is the relationship between the nouns and the verbs in this sentence? This sentence also contains three semicolons. What is the purpose of this punctuation–construction? Why is it necessary?
3. Native speakers of English would never say "women bear on their backs babies." Why? What principle of word order is involved?

III

Read the following statements closely. Then answer the questions:

1. This selection is also descriptive. How does it differ from the description by Clemens? How does it differ from the description you wrote? Does the selection satisfy the basic purpose of description? In what ways does it succeed or fail?
2. In this selection, as in the one by Clemens, a number of examples are used. Here, however, a different type of description is employed. Notice the kind of details used here. What is the principle of organization? Is the reader literally walked through the location, as he was in "My Home Town"?
3. There are literally thousands of details that might have been selected in this case. Why did the writer choose the ones he did? What, if anything, do they contribute to the description?

THEOPHRASTUS

The Unseasonable Man

Unseasonableness is a tendency to do socially permissible things at the wrong time. The unseasonable man is the sort of person who comes to *confide* in you when you are busy. He serenades his girl friend when she is ill. He asks a man who has just lost money by signing a bill for a friend to sign a bill for him. He comes to court to appear as a witness after the trial is over. When he goes to a wedding, he talks against women. He invites a friend to go for a ride just after thc friend has finished a long auto trip. He brings a higher *bidder* to a salesman who has just closed a deal. He tells a long story to people who have heard it many times before. He is eager to offer services which are not wanted but which cannot be politely refused. If he is present at an *arbitration,* he stirs up *dissension* between the two parties, who were really anxious to agree. Such is the *unseasonable* man.

The Grumbler

Grumbling is complaining too much of one's bad fortune. A grumbler is such a person. When his sweetheart smothers him with kisses, he says, "I wish you really liked me that much."

"The Unseasonable Man" and "The Grumbler" are adapted from a work entitled *Characters* (date unknown). Theophrastus was a Greek philosopher, native of Lesbos, and pupil of Aristotle.

He is angry with the Gods, not because it doesn't rain, but because it doesn't rain when he desires that it should. Finding a purse along the street, he says, as he counts the money in it, "Ah, I never find anything worthwhile." If he has *convinced* a merchant to reduce the price of some goods, he will remark, "Anything that cheap must be no good." *Congratulated* on the birth of his son, he replies, "Only one more mouth to feed." When he wins a *lawsuit,* he *reproaches* his *attorney* for having omitted several important points. Once his friends got together to lend him some money. He accepted it, but he was very sad. His friends said, "Come, cheer up, things could be worse." He answered, "Cheer up? How can I? Not only do I have to pay back all the money, but on top of that I have to be grateful to everyone of you." Such is the *grumbler.*

Exercises and Questions for Analysis

I

Define each of the following italicized words as used in the context of the sentence:

1. He comes to *confide* in you when you are busy.
2. He brings a higher *bidder* to a salesman.
3. If he is present at an *arbitration,* he stirs up *dissension* between the two parties.
4. Such is the *unseasonable* man.
5. He has *convinced* a merchant to reduce the price.
6. He is *congratulated* on the birth of his son.
7. When he wins a *lawsuit,* he *reproaches* his *attorney.*
8. Such is the *grumbler.*

II

Answer the following questions:

1. In the first two sentences in both selections, the verb "is" occurs. What kind of verb is it? Why is it used here? Change the verb —not just the tense—but retain the essential meaning.

2. Make two sentences out of the following: "He is angry with the Gods, not because it doesn't rain, but because it doesn't when he desires that it should." Which is the more effective—one sentence, or two? Why?

III

Read the following statements closely, answer the questions, and write the theme assignment:

1. The literary term "character" designates a literary type or set form derived from Theophrastus, an Athenian schoolmaster of the third century B.C. This type does not satisfy the requirements of what is called a "character sketch." Rather the "character" is a caricature not of an individual but of a type. It generalizes. It belongs to the same general class as many editorial cartoons and comic strips. Notice that there is no recognizable description of a person in terms of personal appearance, habit, individual characteristics. Still, certain specific details are included. What are some of the specific details used in these two "characters"? Why are they included? Have you known persons who were guilty of one of these excesses? Have you ever met anyone who was guilty of all of them?

2. The last few selections which you have read were descriptions. However, they were descriptions of physical locations. The "characters" are also descriptive, but of types rather than places. What characteristics do these descriptions have in common with the others? How do they differ? Do "The Unseasonable Man" and "The Grumbler" meet the requirements of good description? How do they succeed or fail?

3. Attempt to write a "character" of your own. Remember that you are not trying to describe a real person, or even an imaginary one, but rather—a human type.

CHARLES DICKENS

Miss Murdstone

Miss Murdstone arrived at our house one evening shortly after dinner. She was a *gloomy looking* woman, dark like her brother, Mr. Murdstone, who was now my step-father. She had dark eyebrows which almost met over her large nose. She brought with her two *uncompromising* black trunks, with her initials on the lids in hard brass nails. When she paid the driver, she took her money out of a hard steel purse, and she kept the purse in *a very jail of a bag* which hung upon her arm by a heavy chain and which *shut up like a bite.* I had never seen such a *metallic* lady as Miss Murdstone.

She was brought into the *parlor* with many tokens of welcome and there formally recognized by my mother as a new and near relation. Then she looked at me and said, "Is that your boy, sister-in-law?"

My mother *acknowledged* me.

"Generally speaking," said Miss Murdstone, "I don't like boys. How do you do, boy?"

Under these circumstances, I replied that I was very well and that I hoped she was well also, but I was so embarrassed and ill at ease that Miss Murdstone was able to dispose of me in two words: "Wants manners," she said.

Having uttered these words with great *distinctness,* she asked to be shown to her room. This room became to me from that time forth a place of awe and dread. Within this room, the two

From *David Copperfield* (1849-50).

black boxes were never seen open or known to be left unlocked. Furthermore, numerous *little steel fetters and rivets,* with which Miss Murdstone *embellished* herself when she dressed up, generally hung around the mirror in formidable array.

Exercises and Questions for Analysis

I

Define each of the following italicized words as used in the context of the sentence. Each phrase in brackets should be defined as a unit:

1. She was a [*gloomy looking*] woman.
2. She had two *uncompromising* black bags.
3. She kept her purse in [*a very jail of a bag*] . . . which [*shut up like a bite*].
4. I had never seen such a *metallic* lady as Miss Murdstone.
5. She was brought into the *parlor.*
6. My mother *acknowledged* me.
7. She uttered these words with great *distinctness.*
8. Numerous [*little steel fetters and rivets*], with which Miss Murdstone *embellished* herself . . . hung around the mirror . . .

II

Answer the following questions:

1. Miss Murdstone's words—in quotation marks—are in a different tense from the author's general remarks and description. What tense are they in? Why doesn't Dickens use the same tense throughout?
2. In what tense is the following sentence: "When she paid the driver, she took her money out of a hard steel purse, and she kept the purse in a very jail of a bag which hung upon her arm by a heavy chain and which shut up like a bite." How do you know the tense? Change this sentence to the future tense.
3. Make two sentences out of the above sentence. Which is the

more effective, one sentence or two? Why? What is the function of the comma after the words "a hard steel purse"?

III

Read the following statements closely, answer the questions, and write the assignment:

1. Unlike the "characters" represented in the last selection, this excerpt is a "character sketch." A "character sketch" does not refer to a human type in caricature, but rather to a developed personality. This passage is still descriptive, but unlike the earlier descriptions, a single person is described rather than a place or type. Notice the amount of specific detail employed. Point out the dominant characteristic of the person described, and indicate the specific details given which contribute to the building up of that characteristic.

2. Since this passage is still descriptive, how does it differ from the other descriptive passages? Does this selection satisfy the basic purposes of description? In what ways does it succeed or fail?

3. Prepare a plan for a character sketch that you might write. Include a number of specific details that you might use to develop a particular characteristic. At the same time, remember to use enough variety to avoid tedium.

SECTION II

Definition

JOHN HENRY NEWMAN

The Definition of a Gentleman

It is almost a definition of a gentleman to say that he is one who never inflicts pain. This description is both refined and, as far as it goes, accurate. He is mainly occupied in merely removing the obstacles which hinder the free action of those about him; and he *concurs* with their movements rather than takes the *initiative* himself. The benefits he provides may be considered to be parallel to what are called comforts or conveniences in the affairs of ordinary life; that is, he is like an *easy chair* or a warm bath, which do their part in easing *fatigue* or providing warmth, though nature provides both means of rest and animal heat without them. The true gentleman carefully avoids whatever may cause a *jolt* in the minds of those with whom he is associated; all clashing of opinion, or collision of feeling, all suspicion, or gloom, or resentment. His great concern is to make everyone feel at ease and at home. He has his eye on all of his company; he is *tender* toward the *bashful, gentle* toward the *distant,* and *merciful* toward the *absurd.* He is always aware of the person to whom he is speaking. He avoids careless *allusions* or irritating topics. He seldom *dominates* a conversation, and he is never a *bore.* He *makes light* of favors while he does them, and he seems to be receiving them while he is conferring them. He has no ear for slander or gossip, and he interprets every-

From *The Idea of a University* (1873).

thing in the best possible light. He never takes unfair advantage, and he never *insinuates* evil which he does not dare to speak out. He has too much good sense to be irritated by insults. He is *patient, forbearing,* and *resigned,* on *philosophical principles.* He is as *simple* as he is *forcible,* and as *brief* as he is *decisive.* He may be right or wrong in his opinions, but he is too *clearheaded* to be *unjust.*

Exercises and Questions for Analysis

I

Define each of the following italicized words as used in the context of the sentence. Each phrase in brackets should be defined as a unit:

1. He *concurs* with their movements.
2. He never takes the *initiative* himself.
3. He is like an [*easy chair*].
4. It does its part in easing *fatigue.*
5. He avoids whatever may cause a *jolt* in someone's mind.
6. He is *tender* toward the *bashful, gentle* toward the *distant,* and *merciful* toward the *absurd.*
7. He avoids careless *allusions.*
8. He seldom *dominates* a conversation.
9. He is never a *bore.*
10. He [*makes light*] of favors.
11. He never *insinuates* evil.
12. He is *patient, forbearing,* and *resigned* on [*philosophical principles*].
13. He is as *simple* as he is *forcible,* and as *brief* as he is *decisive.*
14. He is too *clearheaded* to be *unjust.*

II

Answer the following questions:

1. Make a list of all the adjectives in this selection. Is the list surprisingly long or short?
2. In the sentence "He makes light of favors while he does them . . . ," "makes light" functions as a verb. Conjugate it in the present, past, future, present perfect, and past perfect tenses.
3. In sentence five, what is the function of "all clashing of opinion, or collision of feeling, all suspicion, or gloom, or resentment"?

III

Read the following statements closely, answer the questions, and write the assignment:

1. What is the purpose of a definition? Does this selection satisfy this basic purpose?
2. Notice, particularly in sentences 7, 12, and 13 above, the extreme care which has been employed by the writer in selecting exactly the right words to express himself. In many ways, this "definition" approaches in technique the "character." Notice the specific details and illustrations which are used to expand the definition. What are they?
3. *Webster's Collegiate Dictionary* defines the word "gentleman" in the following manner: "A well-bred man of fine feelings, good education, and social position." How does this definition compare with Newman's? Which is more accurate? Why? Look up the words "denotative" and "connotative" in your own dictionary. Which of these definitions is denotative, Newman's or Webster's? Which is connotative? How do you know?
4. State your personal definition of a gentleman. Does your definition agree or disagree with Newman's? Do you think his definition would be universally accepted? Would you say that his definition is also personal?

HENRI BERGSON

A Definition

The first point to which I would like to call your attention is that nothing comic exists *outside the boundary* of what is strictly human. A landscape may be beautiful, graceful, sublime, insignificant, or ugly; it will never be ludicrous. We may laugh at an animal, but only because we have *detected* in it some human expression or *attitude*. We may laugh at a hat, but we are not laughing at the piece of felt or straw. We are laughing at the shape that men have given to it, the human *whim* whose *mold* it has assumed. I wonder why a fact so important has not attracted the attention of philosophers to a greater degree. Some have defined man as an animal that knows how to laugh. They could equally well have defined him as an animal which provokes laughter; for if any other animal, or some lifeless object, achieves the same effect, it is always because of some *similarity* to man.

Now stand away and look at life as an *unconcerned bystander*. Many dramas will turn into comedies. We only have to stop our ears to the sound of music in a room where dancing is going on for the dancers to appear ridiculous. How many human actions could stand this kind of test? Should we not see many of them suddenly pass from *grave* to pleasant, if we isolate them from the *accompanying music of sentiment?* There-

From *Laughter, An Essay On the Meaning of the Comic* (1900). Translated especially for this edition by Marcel Bolomet, Adjunct Assistant Professor of French, University of Southern California.

fore, in order to produce the whole of its effect, the comic demands something like a momentary *anesthesia* of the heart. It appeals to pure intelligence.

However, this intelligence must remain in contact with other intelligences. There is the third fact to which I wanted to draw attention. We would hardly appreciate the comic if we felt isolated from others. It seems that laughter needs an echo.

Let us clearly mark the point where our three *preliminary observations* are *converging*. The comic will come into being, it seems, when a group of men direct their attention to one of themselves, *imposing* silence on their emotions, and calling into play only their *intelligence*.

Exercises and Questions for Analysis

I

Define each of the following italicized words as used in the context of the sentence. Each phrase in brackets should be defined as a unit:

1. The comic does not exist [*outside the boundary*] of what is strictly human.
2. You have *detected* in it some human expression or *attitude*.
3. It is the human *whim* whose *mold* it has assumed.
4. It is always because of some *similarity* to man.
5. Look at life as an [*unconcerned bystander*].
6. Should we not see many of them suddenly pass from *grave* to pleasant, if we isolate them from the [*accompanying music of sentiment*]?
7. The comic demands a momentary *anesthesia* of the heart.
8. Let us clearly mark the point where our three [*preliminary observations*] are *converging*.

9. The comic will come into being whenever a group of men direct their attention to one of themselves, *imposing* silence on their emotions, and calling into play only their *intelligence.*

II

Answer the following questions:

1. Make a list of all the adverbs in this selection. Is the list very long, or is it short? How do you explain its length?
2. What is the subject of the first sentence? Of the ninth sentence? Of the thirteenth?
3. To whom is this selection addressed? How do you know?

III

Read the following statements closely, answer the questions, and do the assignments:

1. This definition, unlike the preceding one, depends entirely on accurate observation and deduction. Is this a connotative or a denotative definition of the comic? Does this selection satisfy the basic purpose of a definition? To what degree does it succeed or fail?
2. Look up the word "comic" in your dictionary. How does the dictionary definition differ from Bergson's?
3. State your own definition of the comic. How does your definition differ from Bergson's?
4. Write a formal definition of any one of the following terms: beauty, literature, education, intelligence, truth, knowledge, training, democracy.

SECTION III

Classification

OLIVER GOLDSMITH

The Spider

Animals in general are *shrewd* in proportion as they cultivate society. Elephants and beavers show the greatest signs of this sagacity when they are together in large numbers, but when man *invades* their *communities* they lose all their spirit of *industry.*

Among insects, the labors of the bee and the ant have attracted the attention and admiration of naturalists, but all their *sagacity* seems to be lost upon *separation,* and a single bee or ant seems *destitute* of every degree of industry. It becomes the most stupid insect imaginable, and it *languishes* and soon dies.

Of all the solitary insects I have ever noticed, the spider is the most sagacious, and its actions seem almost to exceed belief. This insect is formed by nature for war, not only on other insects, but also on its own species.

Its head and breast are covered with a strong natural *coat of mail,* which is *impenetrable* to the attacks of every other insect. Its body is covered with a soft, *pliable* skin which is safe even from the sting of the wasp. Its legs are *terminated* by strong claws, not unlike those of a lobster.

It has several eyes which are large, *transparent,* and covered with a *horny substance* which does not *impede* the vision. Besides this, it is *furnished* with a *forceps* above the mouth, which serves to kill its *prey.*

Its net, used to *entangle* its enemies, seems to be what it

From *The Bee* (Vol. I, No. 4, 20 Oct. 1759).

chiefly trusts and what it takes most pains to accomplish. Nature has furnished the body of the spider with a *glutinous* liquid which it spins into a thread. In order to fix its thread when it begins to spin, it emits a small drop of its liquid against a hard surface. This liquid, hardening by degrees, serves to anchor the thread firmly. Then, as the spider moves away from the first point, the thread lengthens. When the spider comes to the place where the other end of the thread is to be fixed, it gathers the thread up in its claws and stretches the thread tight and finally fixes it to a solid surface in the same way that it did the original end. And so the spider continues until the web is finished.

The male spiders are much smaller than the female. When the females lay their eggs, they spread a part of the web under the eggs, and then roll them up in it, as we roll things up in a cloth. This roll they carry into their holes. If they are disturbed, they never attempt to escape without carrying their brood with them in their forceps.

As soon as the young ones leave their *artificial covering,* they begin to *spin,* and they grow larger so quickly that one can almost watch them grow.

Exercises and Questions for Analysis

I

Define each of the following italicized words as used in the context of the sentence. Each phrase in brackets should be defined as a unit:

1. Animals in general are *shrewd.*
2. When man *invades* their *communities* they lose all their spirit of *industry.*
3. All their *sagacity* seems to be lost upon *separation.*
4. A single bee or ant seems *destitute* of every degree of industry.

5. It *languishes.*
6. Its head and breast are covered with a [*coat of mail*] which is *impenetrable* to the attacks of other insects.
7. Its body is covered with a soft, *pliable* skin.
8. Its legs are *terminated* by strong claws.
9. Its eyes are large and *transparent.*
10. They are covered with a *horny substance* which does not *impede* the vision.
11. It is *furnished* with a *forceps* above the mouth with which it kills its *prey.*
12. Its net is used to *entangle* its enemies.
13. Nature has furnished the body of the spider with a *glutinous* liquid.
14. As soon as the young ones leave their [*artificial coverings*], they begin to *spin.*

II

Answer the following questions:

1. In the seventh paragraph, the following statement occurs: ". . . The females . . . roll their eggs up in their webs, as we roll things up in a cloth." In this statement, "roll up" is a *phrasal verb.* Go back through the preceding two or three selections and pick out other phrasal verbs. Conjugate these verbs fully.
2. What is the function of the following group of words in the first sentence in paragraph three: "Of all the solitary insects I have ever noticed . . ."
3. In the same sentence, what is the function of the second comma?
4. Make a list of all the prepositional phrases you can find in this selection and identify them according to their functions.

III

Read the following statements and questions closely. Then answer the questions:

1. The process of "classification" is exactly opposite in intent to the process of definition. How? What is the purpose of classification?

2. Does this selection satisfy the requirements of classification? How does it succeed or fail?

3. Notice that this selection, like the one by Bergson, is based almost exclusively on personal observation. Is personal observation sufficient to achieve good definition or classification?

4. On the basis of what you personally know about spiders, would you say that Goldsmith's observation is accurate? Is he a good scientist?

JOSEPH ADDISON

What is a Pedant?

A man who has been brought up among books, and who is able to talk of nothing else, is a very poor companion. He is what we call a *pedant.* But, I think, we should enlarge the title, and give it to everyone who does not know how to think of anything except his profession or his own particular way of life.

Who is a greater pedant than a playboy? *Bar* him from talking about the nightclubs, a catalogue of famous beauties, and an account of a few fashionable illnesses that he has had, and you *strike him dumb.* How many gentlemen are limited to a knowledge of high society and its many parties? Such gentlemen will tell you the names of the important guests, will repeat the *shrewd* sayings of a well-known man, will whisper about an *intrigue* that is not yet common knowledge; or, if the sphere of their observations is a little larger than ordinary, will perhaps enter into all the incidents, turns, and revolutions in a game of poker. When they have gone so far, they have shown you the whole circle of their *accomplishments.* Their abilities are drained, and they are disabled from any further conversation. What are these but rank pedants? And yet these are the men who pride themselves most on their *exemption* from the pedantry of colleges.

I might here mention the military pedant, who always talks about war, and who is storming towns, and fighting battles from one end of the year to the other. Everything he speaks smells

From *The Spectator* (Vol. II, No. 105, 30 June 1711).

of gunpowder. If you take away his artillery, he has not a word to say for himself. I might likewise mention the law pedant, who is *perpetually* explaining cases, repeating the *transactions* of the local Hall of Justice, and *wrangling* with you upon the most unimportant details of life. He can not be convinced of the distance from one place to another, or of the most *trivial* point in any conversation, except by argument.

The state pedant is wrapped up in the news and lost in politics. If you mention either the prime minister of Canada or the Shah of Iran, he talks very much, but if you go beyond the *Times* you lose him.

Of all the *species* of pedants which I have mentioned, the book pedant is the most *tolerable.* He has at least some intelligence and a head which is full, though confused. A man who converses with him may often receive from him hints of things that are worth knowing. An average man may learn from him things he may possibly turn to his own advantage, though they are of little use to the owner. The worst kind of pedants among learned men are those who are naturally gifted with a very small share of common sense, but who have read a great number of books without taste.

The truth of it is that *learning,* like traveling and all other methods of *improvement,* as it provides good sense, so it also makes a silly man ten thousand times more insufferable by supplying variety to his ignorance. Learning brings out wisdom in a wise man and foolishness in a foolish man. In short, a mere playboy, a mere soldier, a mere *scholar,* a mere anything, is an *insipid* pedantic character, and ridiculous.

Exercises and Questions for Analysis

I

Define each of the following italicized words as used in the context of the sentence. Each phrase in brackets should be defined as a unit:

1. He is what we call a *pedant.*
2. *Bar* him from talking about a few special topics, and you [*strike him dumb*].
3. He will repeat *shrewd* sayings.
4. He will whisper about *intrigues.*
5. He has then shown the whole of his *accomplishments.*
6. He prides himself on his *exemption* from pedantry.
7. He repeats the *transactions* of the local Hall of Justice.
8. The law pedant is [*perpetually wrangling*] with you about the most *trivial* points.
9. Of all *species* of pedants, the book pedant is the most *tolerable.*
10. *Learning,* like all other methods of *improvement,* is limited in its value.
11. In short, a mere playboy, a mere *scholar,* a mere anything, is an *insipid* pedantic character.

II

Answer the following questions and write the assignment:

1. In what way does this author classify his material? Point out the specific divisions in the text.
2. In what ways is this classification like Goldsmith's? In what ways is this classification different from Goldsmith's?
3. To what extent does personal observation become important in this selection?
4. Write a paper in which you classify one of the following: bores, teachers, politicians, animals, books, students.

SECTION IV

Process

BENJAMIN FRANKLIN

How to Make Lightning Rods

Prepare a steel rod about five or six feet long, about half an inch thick at its largest end, and tapering to a sharp point. This point should be *gilded* to prevent its rusting. Secure to the big end of the rod a strong eye or a ring half an inch in diameter. Fix the rod upright to the chimney or the highest part of a house. It should be fixed with some sort of *staples* or special nails to keep it steady. The pointed end should extend upward, and should rise three or four feet above the *chimney* or building to which the rod is fixed. Drive into the ground an iron rod about one inch in diameter, and ten or twelve feet long. This rod should also have an *eye* or ring fixed to its upper end. It is best to place the iron rod some distance from the *foundation* of the house. Ten feet away is a good distance, if the size of the *property* permits. Then take as much length of iron rod of a smaller *diameter* as will be necessary to reach from the eye on the rod above to the eye of the rod below. Fasten this securely to the fixed rods by passing it through the eyes and bending the ends to form rings too. Then close all the joints with lead. This is easily done by making a small bag of strong paper around the joints, tying it tight below, and then pouring in the *molten* lead. It is useful to have these joints treated in this way so that there will be a considerable area of contact between each piece. To prevent the wind from shaking this long rod, it may be fastened to the building by several staples. If the building

From a letter to David Hume, dated from London on January 24, 1762.

is especially large or long, extending more than one hundred feet for example, it is wise to erect a rod at each end. If there is a *well* sufficiently near to the building to permit placing the iron rod in the water, this is even better than the use of the iron rod in the ground. It may also be wise to paint the iron to prevent it from *rusting*. A building so *protected* will not be *damaged* by lightning.

Exercises and Questions for Analysis

I

Define each of the following italicized words as used in the context of the sentence:

1. The point should be *gilded*.
2. It should be fixed with some sort of *staple*.
3. It should rise three or four feet above the *chimney*.
4. This rod should also have an *eye* fixed to one end of it.
5. It is best to place the iron rod some distance from the *foundation* of the house.
6. The size of *property* should permit the rod to be at least ten feet away.
7. An iron rod of smaller *diameter* should be used.
8. Then pour in the *molten* lead.
9. A *well* near the building is useful.
10. Paint will prevent *rust*.
11. A building so *protected* will not be *damaged* by lightning.

II

Answer the following questions:

1. Both the fifth sentence and the ninth sentence begin with the word "it," but the structure of the sentences is different.

identify each of the two types of sentences. Find other sentences in the selection which are like the ninth sentence in structure.

2. To whom is this selection addressed? How do you know? What is the subject of many of the sentences, for example—the first?

III

Read the following statements closely, answer the questions, and write the assignment:

1. A "process" is a description of the way in which something is, was, or should be done. If you have ever consulted a cookbook, you have read the description of a process. This type is useful in many ways, as you will see when reading the next selection. Notice that each step is carefully described and presented in order. Pick out and identify each step as described by Franklin. Notice the kinds of sentences he uses. What percentage of these sentences are imperative?
2. Write a paper describing a process that you know well.

THEODOR MOMMSEN

The Roman Funeral

The Roman *funeral* was a remarkable *ceremony*. It was a *procession* to which the citizens were *summoned* by the public *crier:* "That warrior is dead. Whoever can, let them come to *escort* him as he is carried from his house." The procession was opened by bands of wailing women, musicians, and dancers. One of the dancers was dressed up and furnished with a mask in the likeness of the *deceased*. Then came the grandest and most peculiar part of the ceremony: the procession of *ancestors*. This part of the *pageant* so outshone the rest that certain noblemen instructed their *heirs* to restrict the funeral ceremony to this part alone. The chief ornament of a Roman house was the collection of masks of those ancestors who had occupied any high office. These masks, made of wax and often very old, were kept in *niches* along the walls of the family hall. When a death occurred, suitable persons wore these masks in the funeral ceremony.

The dead man lay upon a *bier* spread with fine linen cloths and with various *covers embroidered* in purple and gold. Around him lay the *armor* of the enemies he had killed. Behind the bier came the mourners, all in black, without ornament. The mourners were the sons of the deceased, with veiled faces, the daughters, without veils, and the relatives and friends. Thus the procession passed on to the *Forum*. There the *corpse* was set erect. The ancestors descended from their *chariots* and seated

From *History of Rome* (1854-56). Translated by W. P. Dickson.

themselves in special chairs. The eldest son of the deceased mounted the *rostrum* and announced to the assembled multitude the names and deeds of each of the ancestors and the name and deeds of the newly dead man.

The conception of this funeral ceremony was in keeping with the grave *solemnity* and the proud *dignity* of Roman life.

Exercises and Questions for Analysis

I

Define each of the following italicized words as used in the context of the sentence:

1. The Roman *funeral* was a remarkable *ceremony.*
2. It was a *procession.*
3. The citizens were *summoned* by the public *crier.*
4. "Let them come to *escort* him."
5. A dancer wore a mask in the likeness of the *deceased.*
6. A procession of *ancestors* was part of the ceremony.
7. This part of the *pageant* outshone the rest.
8. Certain noblemen instructed their *heirs* to omit everything else.
9. These masks were kept in *niches.*
10. The dead man lay upon a *bier.*
11. The bier was spread with *covers embroidered* in purple and gold.
12. The *armor* of his enemies lay around him.
13. The procession passed on to the *Forum.*
14. The *corpse* was set erect.
15. The ancestors descended from their *chariots.*
16. The eldest son mounted the *rostrum.*
17. It was in keeping with the grave *solemnity* and the proud *dignity* of Roman life.

II

Answer the following questions:

1. Analyze the structure of the fourth sentence in the second paragraph. What is the function of the two prepositional phrases?
2. In the next to the last sentence in the first paragraph determine the function of the words "made of wax and often very old." Why is this expression set off in commas?
3. In the words spoken by the crier, is "whoever" singular or plural? Why? How do you know?

III

Read the following statements closely, answer the questions, and write the assignment:

1. In this instance, the device known as the "process" has been employed to describe a historical practice. Notice that each step is fully developed with necessary explanation, and that each step is presented in order. Pick out each step of the process.
2. Compare this rather more complex process with the process described by Franklin. How are they different? In what ways are the two selections similar?
3. Write a paper in which you describe a custom of your native country or section of the country. Employ the step by step process.

Review

I. Vocabulary

Define each of the following words in a complete sentence. Then use each of the words in a sentence of your own:

1. pageant
2. drowsed
3. toddlers
4. parlor
5. fatigue
6. prey
7. arbitration
8. damaged
9. crier
10. yelps
11. pliable
12. bore
13. acknowledge
14. reproach
15. droning
16. bier
17. burros
18. confide
19. absurd
20. attitude
21. impede
22. gilded
23. covers
24. diameter
25. invade
26. detect
27. insinuate
28. distinctness
29. bray
30. corpse

II. Special terminology

Define each of the following:

1. character
2. process
3. characterization
4. classification

Distinguish between:

1. denotative and connotative definition
2. character and character sketch
3. definition and classification

III. *Identification*

In a few words identify the following:

1. Samuel L. Clemens
2. Henri Bergson
3. John Henry Newman
4. Oliver Goldsmith
5. Theodor Mommsen
6. Theophrastus
7. Charles Dickens
8. Joseph Addison
9. Benjamin Franklin
10. Miss Murdstone

IV. *Content*

Answer the following questions briefly:

1. What is the principal characteristic of the grumbler?
2. What is the principal characteristic of the town described by Clemens?
3. What specific details do you recall about a Roman funeral?
4. How would you make a lightning rod?
5. What is a gentleman?

V. *Composition*

Write a paper in which you state in detail what you have learned from the first section of this textbook. Include such items as vocabulary, style, grammar, organization, and paragraphing, as well as factual matters you have learned from the content of the selections.

SECTION V

Characterization

JOHN RICHARD GREEN

Queen Elizabeth at Twenty-five

England's one hope at the end of the sixteenth century lay in the character of her Queen. Elizabeth was now in her twenty-fifth year. Personally she was even more beautiful than her mother. Her figure was commanding. Her face was long, but *queenly* and intelligent. Her eyes were quick and fine. She had grown up amid the liberal culture of the Court of Henry VIII. She was a bold rider, a good shot, a graceful dancer, a skillful musician, and an *accomplished scholar.* She inherited from her father her *frank* and *hearty* speech, her love of *popularity,* her courage, and her amazing self-confidence. Her *harsh,* man-like voice, her strong will, her pride, and her bad temper came to her through her Tudor blood. She *scolded* great noblemen as though they were schoolboys. From time to time she interrupted the most serious discussions to *swear* at her counselors. But at the same time she inherited from her mother, Anne Boleyn, a great love of splendor and pleasure. She loved gaiety, and laughter, and wit. She *hoarded* jewels. Her dresses were *innumerable.* Her vanity remained with her even into old age. No *flattery* of her beauty was ever too *exaggerated.*

Yet Elizabeth lived simply and *frugally,* and she worked hard. She was the coolest and hardest of politicians at the council table. She would *tolerate* no flattery from her advisors. She

From *A Short History of the English People* (1874).

listened, she *weighed,* she used or set aside the counsels of each in turn. But her policy as a whole was her own. It was a policy, not of genius, but of good sense. Her aims were simple and obvious. She wanted to *preserve* her *throne,* to keep England at peace, and to *restore civil* order.

If Elizabeth loved anything, she loved England. She once said, "No *worldly* thing *under the sun* is so dear to me as the love and *good-will* of my *subjects.*" This love and good-will she did win.

Exercises and Questions for Analysis

I

Define each of the following italicized words as used in the context of the sentence. The phrase in brackets should be defined as a unit:

1. Her face was *queenly* and intelligent.
2. She was an *accomplished scholar.*
3. Her speech was *frank* and *hearty.*
4. She loved *popularity.*
5. Her voice was *harsh.*
6. She *scolded* great noblemen.
7. She *swore* at her advisors.
8. She *hoarded* jewels.
9. Her dresses were *innumerable.*
10. No *flattery* was too *exaggerated.*
11. Yet she lived *frugally.*
12. She would *tolerate* no flattery from her advisors.
13. She *weighed* the advice of each.

14. She wanted to *preserve* her *throne,* to keep England at peace, and to *restore civil* order.

15. "No *worldly* thing [*under the sun*] is so dear to me as the love and *good-will* of my *subjects.*"

II

Answer the following questions:

1. The third through the sixth sentences in the first paragraph are similar in structure. What kind of verb is used in these sentences? What kind of sentences are these?
2. What is the subject of the tenth sentence?
3. The fourteenth and fifteenth sentences differ from the third and sixth. How?

III

Read the following statements and questions closely. Then answer the questions:

1. Notice the differences between this "characterization" and the "character" and "character-sketch" which appear earlier in this book. The "character" is a description of a human type. The "character-sketch" attempts to bring out only one side of a personality. But a "characterization" attempts to present a "whole" human being, just as this person might be if one were to meet him in real life. Point out at least two specific differences between this characterization and the earlier types.
2. What kind of detail is employed in this selection to give the reader a vivid picture of the character of Elizabeth? Is there a great deal of physical description in this selection? Is there a great deal of what might be called "psychological" description? What is the difference between these two types of description?
3. What is the purpose of characterization? To what degree does this selection succeed or fail in satisfying that purpose? In what other ways does it succeed or fail?

WILLIAM H. HERNDON

Mr. Lincoln

Mr. Lincoln was six feet four inches high. When he left his home for Washington, he was fifty-one years old. He was in good health, and he had little or no grey hair on his head. He was thin, *wiry, rawboned.* He was slightly *stoop-shouldered.* His usual weight was about one hundred and eighty pounds. His general structure was loose and leathery. He had dark skin, dark hair, and always looked sad. He was extremely slow in his movements. The whole man, body and mind, moved slowly, as if it needed oiling. Physically he was a very powerful man, lifting four hundred pounds with ease. One occasion is recorded when he lifted six hundred pounds. His mind, like his body, was slow but strong.

Mr. Lincoln's head was long, and tall from the base of the skull in back and from the eyebrows in front. His forehead rose as it ran back at a low angle, like Henry Clay's, but unlike Daniel Webster's. The size of his hat was seven and one-eighth. His forehead was narrow but high. His hair, which was almost black, lay floating where his fingers or a stray wind might have left it. His cheek-bones were high, sharp, and prominent. His jaws were long and upcurved. His nose was large, long, blunt, and a little *awry* towards the right eye. His chin was sharp and uncurved. His eyebrows *cropped out* like a huge rock on the brow of a hill. His long, *sallow* face was wrinkled and dry, with a *mole* here and there. His cheeks were *leathery.* His ears were

From *Herndon's Lincoln: The True Story of a Great Life* (1889).

large and ran out almost at right angles from his head. His lower lip was thick, hanging, and undercurved. His neck was neat and trim.

Thus stood, walked, acted, and looked Abraham Lincoln. He was not a pretty man by any means, nor was he an ugly one. He was a *homely* man, careless of his appearance, plain-looking, and plain-acting. He had no pomp, display, or dignity. He appeared simple in his bearing. He was a sad-looking man. His apparent gloom impressed his friends and created sympathy for him. He was gloomy, *abstracted,* and *humorous by turns.*

His ability to associate ideas was as great as his memory was strong. His language indicated originality of *point of view* as well as of expression. In the search for words, Lincoln was often *at a loss.* He was often *perplexed* to give proper expression to his ideas. This helps to account for his frequent use of stories, *maxims,* and jokes in which to dress his ideas so that they might be more clearly seen.

The great *predominating elements* of Mr. Lincoln's peculiar character were: first, his great *capacity* and power of *reason;* second, his *conscience* and his excellent understanding; third, an *exalted* idea of the sense of right; fourth, his *intense veneration* of the true and the good. But he lived and acted from the standard of reason.

Exercises and Questions for Analysis

I

Define each of the following italicized words as used in the context of the sentence. Each phrase in brackets should be defined as a unit:

1. He was thin, *wiry, rawboned.*
2. He was slightly [*stoop-shouldered*].

3. His nose was a little *awry.*
4. His eyebrows [*cropped out*].
5. His long, *sallow* face was wrinkled and dry, with a *mole* here and there.
6. His cheeks were *leathery.*
7. He was a *homely* man.
8. He was gloomy, *abstracted,* and [*humorous by turns*].
9. His language indicated originality of [*point of view*].
10. Lincoln was often [*at a loss*].
11. He was often *perplexed.*
12. He frequently used stories, *maxims,* and jokes.
13. The great *predominating elements* of Mr. Lincoln's peculiar character were: first, his great *capacity* and power of *reason;* second, his *conscience* and his excellent understanding; third, an *exalted* idea of the sense of right; fourth, his *intense veneration* of the true and the good.

II

Answer the following questions:

1. In the second sentence, what is the function of the expression "When he left his home for Washington"?
2. In the eleventh sentence, what is the function of the expression "lifting four hundred pounds with ease"?
3. In the fifth sentence in the second paragraph, what is the function of the phrase "which was almost black"?

III

Read the following statements closely, answer the questions, and write the assignment:

1. Notice how this selection differs from the one describing the young Elizabeth. There is a great deal more physical description here, and a great deal less psychological description. This can be accounted for partially by the fact that Herndon's point is to contrast Lincoln's unattractive physical exterior with his great mind and spirit. Point out the exact terms used to create

this physical picture of Lincoln. What sorts of words does Herndon use to create his impression? List them.

2. In spite of the abundance of physical detail, this is clearly a "characterization." What makes it so?
3. If this is a characterization, to what degree does it succeed or fail as such, and in what ways does it succeed or fail in general?
4. Write a characterization of someone you know well—but not personally. A teacher or a public figure often makes a good subject.

SECTION VI

Formal Analysis

WALTER PATER

The Mona Lisa

The Mona Lisa is Leonardo da Vinci's *masterpiece.* It is the revealing instance of his *mode* of thought and work. We all know the face and hands of the figure, seated in a marble chair, in a circle of fantastic rocks, illuminated by a light which seems to be some *faint* light under the sea. Perhaps of all ancient pictures, time has *chilled* this one least.

What was the relationship of a living sixteenth century Florentine woman to this creature of Leonardo da Vinci's thought? That there is much of mere *portraiture* in this painting is *attested* by the *legend* that the *subtle* expression of the face was *protracted* by the artificial means of having musicians playing during the *sittings.*

The presence that rose thus so strangely beside the waters is expressive of what, in the course of a thousand years, men had come to desire. The woman in the painting has the head upon which all "the ends of the world are come." Her eyelids are a little weary. Hers is a beauty created outwardly from within. It is composed of the deposit, little cell by cell, of strange thoughts, *reveries,* and *passions.* Set it for a moment beside one of those white Greek goddesses of antiquity. How they would be troubled by this beauty. That face has been *etched* with all the thoughts and experiences of the world, from the earliest days of Greek civilization through the time in which the portrait was painted. She is older than the rocks among

From *Studies in the History of the Renaissance* (1873).

which she sits. The *fancy* of a *perpetual* life, bringing together ten thousand experiences, is an old one. Modern philosophy has conceived the idea of humanity as worked upon, and as summing up within itself, all modes of thought and life. Certainly Mona Lisa might stand as the *embodiment* of that old fancy and the symbol of the modern idea.

Exercises and Questions for Analysis

I

Define each of the following italicized words as used in the context of the sentence:

1. The Mona Lisa is da Vinci's *masterpiece.*
2. It is the revealing instance of his *mode* of thought.
3. It is illuminated by a *faint* under-sea light.
4. Time has *chilled* this painting very little.
5. That there is much of mere *portraiture* in this painting is *attested* by the *legend* that the *subtle* expression was *protracted* by artificial means during the *sittings.*
6. Her beauty is composed of strange thoughts, *reveries,* and *passions.*
7. That face has been *etched* with all the thoughts and experiences of the world, from the earliest days of Greek civilization through the time in which the portrait was painted.
8. The *fancy* of a *perpetual* life is an old one.
9. Mona Lisa might stand as the *embodiment* of that old fancy.

II

Answer the following questions:

1. What is the tense of the first paragraph? Why? Does the tense change in the second paragraph? Why? To what?
2. What is the subject of the sixth sentence, and what is the function of the following group of words: ". . . that the subtle ex-

pression of the face was protracted by the artificial means of having musicians playing during the sittings."

3. In the group of words quoted above, there are a number of prepositional phrases. Identify the function of each.
4. What is the subject of the twelfth sentence?
5. What kind of sentence is the thirteenth? Why is it employed here?

III

Read the following statements and questions closely, answer the questions, and write the assignment:

1. This is an extremely complex passage. It is, of course, an analysis of a painting; thus, it involves not only the mechanics of analysis, but the complexity of art criticism. In this analysis there is a basic underlying assumption about the nature of art. Can you discover and grasp that assumption?
2. What is the purpose of analysis? To what extent does this selection succeed or fail in meeting that purpose? In what other ways does it succeed or fail?
3. In what ways does "analysis" differ from any of the other forms which you have studied? In what ways is it similar to any of the other forms?
4. Pater is captivated by the mystery and magic he finds in this painting. Examine a copy of the painting and then write a paragraph in which you either agree or disagree with Pater's position.

THOMAS BABINGTON MACAULAY

London

Whitehall, when Charles the Second lived there (1660-1685), was the *focus* of political *intrigue* and of fashionable gaiety. Whoever could make himself agreeable to the king or could secure the attention of his mistress might hope to rise in the world without rendering any service to the government, and without even being known by sight to any minister of state. This person got command of a ship, that man got a military commission, a third man got a pardon for a rich criminal, and a fourth man got a lease on government land on easy terms. If the king *proclaimed* that an unknown lawyer should be made a judge or that a drunken *baronet* should be made a *peer*, the *gravest* counselors, after a little murmuring, submitted to the royal will. Interest, therefore, drew a constant crowd of *petitioners* to the gates of the palace, and those gates always stood open. The king kept open house every day and all day long for the good society of London. Hardly any gentleman had any difficulty in making his way into the royal presence. Some *men of quality* came every morning to stand around their master, to chat with him while his *wig* was combed and his necktie was tied, and to accompany him in his early walk through the park. All persons who had been properly introduced might, without special invitation, go to see the king dine, dance, or play cards. They might even have the pleasure of hearing him tell stories.

From *The History of England from the Accession of James the Second* (1849-61).

Whitehall naturally became the chief center for news. Whenever there was a rumor that anything important had happened or was about to happen, people *hastened* to Whitehall to obtain information from the source. There were, however, subjects concerning which information was asked and given in whispers. Men tried to *read the face* of every minister as he went through the *throng.* All sorts of guesses were drawn from the tone in which His Majesty spoke to some person, and in a few hours the hopes and fears inspired by such slight indications had spread to all the coffee-houses in the city.

The coffee-house was a most important political *institution.* After all, no Parliament had sat for years. Public meetings and the rest of the modern machinery of agitation had not yet come into fashion. Nothing resembling the modern newspaper existed. In such circumstances, the coffee-houses were the chief organs through which the public opinion of the city *vented* itself.

The first of these coffee-houses had been established during the time of the Commonwealth (1644-1653). The fashion spread fast. By this time, every man of the upper or middle class went daily to his coffee-house to learn the news and to discuss it. Foreigners remarked that the coffee-house was the thing which especially distinguished London from all other cities; that the coffee-house was the Londoner's second home.

Yet every rank and profession and every shade of religious and political opinion had its own headquarters. There were houses where gentlemen who prided themselves on the beauty of their clothes congregated. There were houses for literary persons. There were coffee-houses where the leading medical men might be consulted. There were Puritan coffee-houses, Jew coffee-houses, and Catholic coffee-houses.

These *gregarious* habits had no small share in forming the character of the Londoner of that age. He was indeed a completely different person from the rural Englishman.

Exercises and Questions for Analysis

I

Define each of the following italicized words as used in the context of the sentence. Each phrase in brackets should be defined as a unit:

1. Whitehall was the *focus* of political *intrigue.*
2. If the king *proclaimed* that a drunken *baronet* should be made a *peer,* the *gravest* counselors submitted to the royal will.
3. Interest drew a constant crowd of *petitioners* to the palace gates.
4. Some [*men of quality*] came every morning to chat with the king while his *wig* was combed and his necktie was tied.
5. People *hastened* to Whitehall to obtain information.
6. Men tried to [*read the face*] of every minister as he went through the *throng.*
7. The coffee-house was a most important political *institution.*
8. The public opinion of the city *vented* itself through the coffee-houses.
9. These *gregarious* habits helped to shape the character of the Londoner.

II

Answer the following questions:

1. What is the function of the following group of words in the first sentence: ". . . when Charles the Second lived there . . ."?
2. Can the third sentence be broken up into more than one sentence? If so, break it up as you think it should be divided. Which is the more effective construction—one or more than one sentence?
3. In the fifth sentence the word "therefore" is set off by commas. Is this punctuation necessary?
4. What difference in meaning would result if the third sentence in the fourth paragraph were rewritten in the following manner: "By this time, every man of the upper or middle class went daily, to his coffee house, to learn the news and to discuss it."

III

Read the following statements closely, answer the questions, and write the assignment:

1. In this selection, Macaulay analyzes the structure of London society during the last half of the seventeenth century. He does so by supplying a miscellany of impressions. These are logically arranged, and the analysis gives the reader a relatively good picture of life in London at that time. No synthesis is provided, however, for the reader is permitted to make his own. (First distinguish clearly between analysis and synthesis. Then decide whether Macaulay's method is preferable to one which provides a synthesis for the reader.)
2. Notice that the general logical movement within the selection is from general statement to specific detail. For example, notice the passage "Whoever could make himself agreeable to the king or could secure the attention of his mistress might hope to rise in the world. . . ." This is a general statement. It is followed by six specific examples of ways in which such persons could rise in the world. Locate other similar rhetorical units.
3. There are three clear and distinct divisions in this passage. Mark each of the three divisions, and note the sentences which serve as transitions between the divisions.
4. Compare this selection with Pater's. Pater bases his analysis on an assumption about the nature of art. Is there an underlying assumption on which Macaulay is building? What is it? What leads you to believe that there is one?
5. To what extent does this analysis satisfy the requirements of the form? In what ways does it succeed or fail?
6. Write a formal analysis of a place you know well, perhaps your native city or country, in which you attempt to analyze the customs and to present a clear view of the life of that place to the reader.

JOSEPH ADDISON

Superstitions

When I went to dine with an old friend, I found his whole family in a state of *dejection.* I asked him the reason for it, and he told me that his wife had a very strange dream the night before, which they were afraid *portended* some *misfortune* to the family. When his wife came into the room, I observed that she was very *melancholy.* I assumed the melancholy to be the result of her dream. As soon as we sat down to dinner, she observed me very carefully. Soon she turned to her husband and said, "My dear, this is the stranger who was in the candle last night."* Soon after this, as they began to talk of family affairs, her son remarked that he was to go to dancing school on Thursday. "Thursday," said she; "No child, if it please God you shall not go on *Childermas* day. Tell your teacher that Friday will be soon enough." I began to reflect on the strangeness of her idea, and to wonder at the fact that anyone would establish a rule to lose a day every week. In the midst of my *musings* she asked me to pass her the salt. I did it in such haste that I dropped the shaker and spilled some salt. She jumped, and said that it fell towards her. I looked rather blank, but I observed that everyone was in a state of concern. I began to consider myself to be a person who had brought disaster upon the whole family. However, the lady recovered herself after a mo-

From *The Spectator* (Vol. I, No. 7, 8 March 1711).

* Dripping wax from a candle was supposed to predict the future.

ment, and said to her husband with a sigh, "My dear, misfortunes never come singly."

My friend, I discovered, played but a small part in his own home. He was a man of more good nature than intelligence, and therefore considered himself *obliged* to agree with the *whims* of his wife. "Do you remember," continued the wife, "that the pigeon-house fell down on the very day that our careless serving maid spilled salt on the table?"

The reader may easily guess that I was quite embarrassed after this incident. I ate as rapidly as I could. To my utter dismay, as I finished eating, the lady saw that I had crossed my knife and fork on my plate. She asked me to humor her and take them out of that figure and place them side by side. I had no idea what I had done wrong, but I suppose it involved some superstition. In obedience to the wishes of the lady, I immediately uncrossed them and laid them down again parallel to each other.

It is not difficult for a man to see that a person has taken a dislike to him. It was perfectly obvious to me, from the looks the lady gave me, that she considered me a very peculiar fellow. In view of this obvious fact, I left immediately after dinner and returned to my own apartment.

When I returned home, I fell into serious *reflection* on the evils that attend these *superstitious follies of mankind.* I thought about the ways in which they subject us to imaginary problems and additional sorrows that do not really concern us. As if the natural *calamities* of life were not enough, we turn the most trivial circumstances into misfortunes, and suffer as much from imaginary accidents as from real evils. I have known a *shooting star* to spoil a night's rest, and I have seen a *grown man* grow pale and lose his appetite over the breaking of a *wishbone.* A screech owl at night has alarmed a family more than a band of robbers; the voice of a cricket has struck more terror than the roaring of a lion.

As it is the chief concern of wise men to *reduce* the evils of life by reasoning, so it is the employment of fools to multiply these evils by *superstitions*.

Exercises and Questions for Analysis

I

Define each of the following italicized words as used in the context of the sentence. Each phrase in brackets should be defined as a unit:

1. I found his whole family in a state of *dejection.*
2. Her dream *portended* some *misfortune.*
3. I observed that she was very *melancholy.*
4. You shall not go on *Childermas* day.
5. In the midst of my *musings* she asked me to pass her the salt.
6. He felt *obliged* to agree with the *whims* of his wife.
7. I fell into serious *reflection* on the evils that attend these [*superstitious follies of mankind*].
8. The natural *calamities* of life are not enough.
9. I have known a [*shooting star*] to spoil a night's rest.
10. I have seen a [*grown man*] grow pale and lose his appetite over the breaking of a *wishbone.*
11. As it is the chief concern of wise men to *reduce* the evils of life by reasoning, so it is the employment of fools to multiply these evils by *superstition.*

II

Answer the following questions:

1. What is the referent for the pronoun "it" in the second sentence?
2. What would happen if the infinitive "to be" in the sentence "I began to consider myself to be a person who had brought disaster upon the whole family," were removed? What would

happen if a comma were inserted before "who had brought"? What is the reason for the use of the past perfect tense in the last part of the sentence?

3. In the third sentence in the fifth paragraph why is the verb "were" employed? Analyze this sentence fully, being sure to account for the verb sequence.

III

Read the following statements closely, answer the questions, and write the assignment:

1. This selection is an analysis of the evils of superstition. What is the tone employed by Addison? What is the purpose of this tone? What does it accomplish?
2. This selection clearly divides into two parts. Indicate the point of division. What is the form of the first part? How does the first part compare with other examples of the same form?
3. Compare this selection with the two preceding ones. How is it similar? How does it differ?
4. In both of the preceding selections of analysis, there was an identifiable but unstated basic assumption underlying much of what the writer had said. Is there such an assumption in this essay? If there is, what is it? What specific details in the selection lead you to believe that you are right?
5. To what extent does this selection succeed or fail in meeting the basic requirements of analysis? In what other ways does it succeed or fail?
6. Write an essay in which you analyze a motion picture or a television program which you have seen recently. Employ everything you have learned about the methods of analysis.

SECTION VII

Comparison and Contrast

EDWARD GIBBON

Rome Under the Tyranny

If a man were asked to name the period in the history of the world when the *condition of the human race* was most happy and prosperous, he would, without hesitation, name that period which elapsed from the death of *Domitian* to the accession of *Commodus* (95-180 A.D.). The vast extent of the Roman empire was governed by absolute power, under the guidance of virtuous and wise men. The Roman armies were restrained by the firm but gentle hand of four successive emperors whose characters and authority commanded *involuntary* respect. The forms of the civil administration were carefully preserved by *Nerva, Trajan, Hadrian,* and the *Antonines,* who delighted in *the image of liberty,* and were pleased to consider themselves *the accountable ministers of the laws.* Such princes deserved the honor of restoring the republic, had the Romans of their day been capable of enjoying *rational freedom.*

The labors of these monarchs were overpaid by the immense reward that came with their success. They were rewarded by the honest pride of virtue, and by the exquisite delight of beholding the general happiness which they had created. A *just* but melancholy *reflection embittered,* however, the noblest of human enjoyments. They must often have *considered* the *instability* of a happiness which depended on the character of a single man. The fatal moment was perhaps approaching when some *immoral* youth, or some *jealous tyrant,* would abuse, to

From *The Decline and Fall of the Roman Empire* (1776-88).

the destruction, that absolute power, which they had exerted for the benefit of their people. The ideal restraints of the senate and the laws might serve to display the virtues, but could never correct the vices, of the emperor.

These gloomy *fears* had already been justified by the experiences of the Romans. The histories of the emperors exhibit a strong and various picture of human nature which one would seek vainly among the mixed and doubtful characters of modern history. (The golden age of Trajan and the Antonines had been preceded by an age of iron.) In the conduct of those earlier monarchs one may trace the utmost lines of vice and virtue, the most exalted perfection, and the meanest degeneracy of our own species. It is almost superfluous to enumerate the unworthy successors of Augustus. Their *unparalleled* vices, and the splendid setting against which they were acted, have saved them from *oblivion.* The dark, *unrelenting Tiberius,* the *furious Caligula,* the *feeble Claudius,* the *profligate* and cruel *Nero,* the *beastly Vitellius,* and the *timid, inhuman Domitian,* are condemned to everlasting *infamy.* During eighty years (excepting only the short and doubtful *respite* of *Vespasian's reign*) Rome *groaned* beneath an *unremitting tyranny* which *exterminated* the ancient families of the republic and was fatal to almost every virtue and every talent that arose in that unhappy period.

Under the reign of those monsters, the slavery of the Romans was accompanied with two peculiar circumstances, the one *occasioned* by their *former* liberty, the other by their extensive conquests, which rendered their condition more completely wretched than that of the victims of tyranny in any other age or country. From these causes were *derived:* 1. the *exquisite sensibility* of the sufferers. 2. the impossibility of escaping from the hand of the oppressor.

1. Persia was once governed by the descendants of Sefi, a race of princes whose wanton cruelty often stained their couch, their table, and their bed with the blood of their favorites.

There is a saying, recorded of a young nobleman, that he never departed from the sultan's presence without satisfying himself whether his head was still on his shoulders. The experience of every day might almost justify the *skepticism* of a Persian. Yet the fatal sword, suspended above him by a single thread, seems not to have disturbed the slumber or interrupted the tranquillity of the Persian. The monarch's frown, he well knew, could level him with the dust. But a stroke of lightning or *apoplexy* might be equally fatal, and it was the *part* of a wise man to forget the *inevitable calamities* of human life in the enjoyment of *the fleeting hour.* He was dignified with the title of the king's slave. He had, perhaps, been purchased from obscure parents, in a country which he had never known, and he was trained up from his infancy in the severe *discipline* of the *seraglio.* His name, his wealth, his honors, were all the gifts of a master who might, without injustice, resume what he had bestowed. His language didn't provide words for any form of government except absolute monarchy. The history of the East informed him that such had always been the condition of mankind. The Koran, and the interpreters of that divine book, taught him that the sultan was the descendant of the prophet and the viceregent of heaven; that patience was the first virtue of a Moslem, and that unlimited obedience was the great duty of a subject.

The minds of the Romans were very differently prepared for slavery. *Oppressed* beneath the weight of their own *corruption* and of military violence, for a long while they preserved the sentiments, or at least the ideas, of their free-born ancestors. From *Grecian philosophy,* they had learned the justest and most liberal *notions* of the dignity of human nature and of the origin of civil society. The history of their own country had taught them to revere a free, virtuous, and victorious commonwealth, and to abhor the successful crimes of Caesar and Augustus. As magistrates and senators, they were admitted into the great council which had once dictated laws to the earth. Its name still gave a *sanction* to the acts of the *monarch*, but its authority was often prostituted to the vilest purposes of tyranny. Tiberius, and those emperors who *adopted* his *maxims*, attempted to disguise their murders by the formalities of justice, and perhaps they enjoyed a secret pleasure in rendering the senate their accomplice as well as their victim. By this assembly, the last of the Romans were condemned for imaginary crimes and real virtues.

2. The division of modern Europe into a number of independent states, connected to each other by the general resemblance of religion, language, and manners, is productive of the most *beneficial consequences* to the liberty of mankind. A modern tyrant who finds no resistance either in his own conscience or in his people, would soon experience a gentle restraint from the example of his equals, from the dread of present censure, from the advice of his allies, and from the fear of his enemies. A political enemy, escaping from the narrow limits of his dominions and going to a neighboring country, could easily obtain a secure refuge and a new *fortune adequate* to his *merit*, the freedom of complaint, and perhaps the means of revenge.

But the empire of the Romans filled the world, and when that empire fell into the hands of a single person, the world became a safe and dreary prison for his enemies. The slave of the Emperor, whether he was condemned to drag his gilded chain in Rome and the senate, or to wear out a life of exile on the frozen banks of the Danube, accepted his fate in silent despair. To resist was fatal. It was impossible to fly. On every side he was surrounded by a *vast extent* of sea and land which he could never hope to *traverse* without being discovered, seized, and restored to his irritated master. Beyond the *frontiers*, his anxious view could discover nothing except the ocean, *inhospitable* deserts, *hostile tribes* of *barbarians*, or dependent kings who would gladly purchase the emperor's protection by the sacrifice of an *obnoxious fugitive.* "Wherever you are," said *Cicero* to the *exiled Marcellus,* "remember that you are equally within the power of the conqueror."

Exercises and Questions for Analysis

I

Define each of the italicized words as used in the context of the sentence. Each phrase in brackets should be defined as a unit:

1. [*The condition of the human race*] was most happy and prosperous between 96 and 180 A.D.
2. The character and authority of these emperors commanded *involuntary* respect.
3. The forms of the civil administration were carefully preserved by *Nerva, Trajan, Hadrian,* and the *Antonines,* who delighted in [*the image of liberty*].
4. They were pleased to consider themselves [*the accountable ministers of the law*].
5. The Romans of their days were not capable of enjoying [*rational freedom*].
6. A *just* but melancholy *reflection embittered* their happiness.
7. They often *considered* the *instability* of their happiness.
8. Some *immoral* youth, or some *jealous tyrant,* could abuse that absolute power.
9. These gloomy *fears* had already been justified by the experiences of the Romans.
10. Their *unparalleled* vices have saved them from *oblivion.*
11. The dark, *unrelenting Tiberius,* the *furious Caligula,* the *feeble Claudius,* the *profligate* and cruel *Nero,* the *beastly Vitellius,* and the *timid, inhuman Domitian* are condemned to everlasting *infamy.*
12. During eighty years (excepting only the short *respite* of *Ves-*

pasian's reign) Rome *groaned* beneath an *unremitting tyranny* which *exterminated* the ancient families of the republic.

13. One peculiar circumstance was *occasioned* by their *former* liberty.
14. From these causes was *derived* the *exquisite sensibility* of the sufferers.
15. The experience might justify the *skepticism* of a Persian.
16. A stroke of lightning or *apoplexy* might be equally fatal.
17. It was the *part* of a wise man to forget the *inevitable calamities* of human life in the enjoyment of [*the fleeting hour*].
18. He was trained up in the severe *discipline* of the *seraglio.*
19. They were *oppressed* beneath the weight of their own *corruption.*
20. From [*Grecian philosophy*] they learned just *notions* of human dignity.
21. Its name still gave a *sanction* to the acts of the *monarch.*
22. Certain emperors *adopted* the *maxims* of Tiberius.
23. The division of modern Europe is productive of the most *beneficial consequences* to liberty.
24. A political enemy may find a new *fortune adequate* to his *merits.*
25. On every side he was surrounded by a *vast extent* of sea and land.
26. He could never hope to *traverse* it.
27. Beyond the *frontier* there were *inhospitable* deserts, *hostile tribes* of *barbarians,* or dependent kings who would gladly purchase the emperor's protection by the sacrifice of an *obnoxious fugitive.*
28. "Wherever you are," said *Cicero* to the [*exiled Marcellus*], "remember that you are equally within the power of the conqueror."

II

Answer the following questions:

1. Notice the sequence of verbs in the first sentence: "were asked, was, would name, elapsed." Explain why each of these verbs is used—that is, justify the tense of each verb.

2. Why is there a tense shift in the first two sentences in the third paragraph?
3. What would be the effect of removing the commas around the phrase "or at least the ideas" in the second sentence in the sixth paragraph?
4. Carefully analyze the structure of the last sentence in the seventh paragraph.
5. Explain the reason for the use of "but" as the first word in the last paragraph.

III

Read the following statement closely. Then answer the questions:

1. This selection employs the method of "comparison and contrast"; that is, in order to explain one process or series of events, that process or series of events is compared with another. In this selection, three different comparisons and contrasts are made. What are the three groups of things compared? How are they compared? Indicate the various divisions of the selection.

The Outline

Now that you have read a number of selections and have improved your comprehension of American English idiom and structure, it is necessary to interrupt the series of selections in order to introduce a discussion of the outline.

The outline, as it shall be discussed here, is merely a discipline intended to assist the student in grasping the significant points of another's writings or lectures, and in improving the structure of his own writing. The human being is a more or less logical animal, and he has become accustomed to receiving information in a more or less orderly sequence. The outline is simply a device which permits one to extract the orderly sequence and examine it independently.

When a carpenter builds a house, he employs a plan for the house. The more intricate the structure, the more detailed the plan must be. But the plan is only a plan. One cannot live in a plan. The house must be built too. This is essentially the relationship between the outline and the finished essay. The outline is a plan for the essay. It is, if one may shift the metaphor, like the skeleton of the essay. It provides the bones, the framework, on which the rest of the structure hangs. The writer then must add the flesh and blood to the basic framework or skeleton. When he has done so, then he will have created a living piece of prose.

The outline should contain several basic items. First, it must have a *topic sentence.* The topic sentence is a *one* sentence statement of the basic idea, the dominant idea, of the whole work. Furthermore, the outline should contain a number of subdivisions of the main idea. Again, a metaphor may be helpful to understand the structure of the outline.

Consider that the topic sentence is a five-dollar bill. It then logically follows that each of the major subdivisions of the selection will be one-dollar bills. For convenience, these subdivisions are marked by Roman numerals. Further subdivisions will logically be into half-dollars (fifty cents), designated by capital letters; quarters (twenty-five cents), designated by arabic numerals; and nickels (five cents), designated by lower-case letters.

Topic Sentence: $5.00

I. $1.00

   A. .50

   B. .50

      1. .25

      2. .25

         a. .05

         b. .05

         c. .05

         d. .05

         e. .05

II. $1.00

III. $1.00

IV. $1.00

V. $1.00

Obviously, each subdivision is equal to every other subdivision at the same level; thus, Roman numeral I is equal in importance to Roman numerals II, III, IV, and V, and capital letter A is equal in importance to capital letter B, and so on. In addition, each group of subdivisions add back up to the next immediate superior item; thus, items a through e, each equal to five cents, total twenty-five cents, the value of item 2, and by the same token items a through e in a normal outline, each equal to the others, total up to item 2 in importance. Furthermore, it should be perfectly obvious, logically as well as in terms of the illustration, that nothing may be divided into fewer than two parts; that is, it is impossible to have a Roman numeral I and no other Roman numerals. There may be as many Roman numerals as the essay demands, but there can be no fewer than two. The same thing is true of all other subdivisions. There must be at least two capital letter items; there may be more, but there cannot be fewer than two. There must be at least two arabic numeral items, and two lower-case letter items. There is no need, in every case, to subdivide that far, but if a subdivision is made, it is necessary to remember that nothing can be subdivided into fewer than two parts.

Perhaps the easiest way to demonstrate how the outline works is to return to the last essay and outline it.

Rome under the Tyranny

Topic Sentence: Under the reign of Tiberius, Caligula, Claudius, Nero, Vitellius, and Domitian, the slavery of the Romans was accompanied by two peculiar circumstances, the one occasioned by their former liberty, the other by their extensive conquests, which rendered their condition more completely wretched than that of the victims of tyranny in any other age or country, and from these causes were derived the exquisite sensibility of the sufferers, and the impossibility of escaping from the hand of the oppressor.

Introduction: If a man were asked to name the period in the history of the world when the condition of the human race was most happy and prosperous, he would, without hesitation, name that period which elapsed from the death of Domitian to the accession of Commodus, but the golden age of Trajan and the Antonines had been preceded by an age of iron.

A. The vast extent of the Roman empire had been ruled by virtuous and wise men.

1. The labors of these monarchs were overpaid by immense rewards.

2. But they must often have considered the instability of a happiness which depended on the character of a single man.

B. These gloomy apprehensions had already been justified by the experience of the Romans.

1. It is almost superfluous to enumerate the unworthy successors of Augustus.

2. During eighty years Rome groaned under an unremitting tyranny.

I. The exquisite sensibility of the sufferers was derived from the former liberty of the Romans.

A. The Persian had been always accustomed to tyranny.

B. The minds of the Romans were differently prepared for slavery.

1. From Grecian Philosophy they had learned just and liberal notions of human dignity.

2. The history of their own country had taught them to revere a free, virtuous, and victorious commonwealth.

II. The impossibility of escaping from the hand of the oppressor was derived from the extensive conquests of the Romans.

A. The division of modern Europe into a number of independent states, connected to each other by the general resemblance of religion, language, and manners, is productive of the most beneficial consequences to the liberty of mankind.

B. But the empire of the Romans filled the world, and when that empire fell into the hands of a single person, the world became a safe and dreary prison for his enemies.

This is a relatively detailed outline of the preceding selection. It is important to notice that, although the topic sentence appears first in the outline, it does not necessarily appear first in the finished work. Notice too that there is no objection to using the exact words of the original in extracting the outline. If the original writer has been kind enough to provide a fine topic sentence, there is no reason why that sentence should not be quoted in the outline. Study the relationship between this outline and the selection from which it is derived. Try to understand clearly the relationship between the various parts of the outline.

Exercises

I

Identify the topic sentences in these preceding selections:

"The Market at Toluca"

"The Definition of a Gentleman"

"The Unseasonable Man" and "The Grumbler"

"Superstitions"

II

Outline the following selections:

"A Definition" (by Henri Bergson)

"How to Make Lightning Rods"

III

Outline your own last theme.

ANTHONY TROLLOPE

The Englishman and the American

The American, though he dresses like an Englishman, and eats roast beef with a fork as does an Englishman, is not like an Englishman in his mind, in his *aspirations,* in his *tastes,* or in his politics.

In his mind he is quicker, more universally intelligent, more ambitious of general knowledge, less *indulgent* of *stupidity* and ignorance in others, harder, sharper, brighter with the surface brightness of steel, than is an Englishman. But, he is more *brittle,* less enduring, less *malleable,* and I think less capable of impressions. The mind of the Englishman has more imagination, but that of the American has more *incision.* The American is a great observer, but he observes things material rather than things social or picturesque.

In his aspirations the American is more constant than the Englishman; that is, he is more constant in aspiring. Every citizen of the United States intends to do something. Everyone thinks himself capable of some effort. But in his aspirations he is more limited than the Englishman. The ambitious American never reaches so high as the ambitious Englishman.

In his tastes the American imitates the Frenchman. Who shall dare to say that he is wrong, seeing that in general matters of design and luxury the French have won for themselves an in-

From *North America* (1862).

ternational *reputation?* I will not say that the American is wrong, but I cannot avoid thinking so. I detest what is called French taste, but the world is against me. When I complained to the landlord of a hotel out in the west that his furniture was useless, he answered me completely by telling me that his house had been furnished not in accordance with the taste of England, but with that of France. I *acknowledged* the *rebuke,* gave up my pursuits of literature and cleanliness, and hurried out of the house as quickly as I could. The taste of America is becoming French in its conversation, French in its comforts, French in its discomforts, French in its eating, French in its dress, French in its manners, and will become French in its art. There are those who say that English taste is taking the same direction. I do not think so. And, therefore, I say that an Englishman and an American differ in their tastes.

But of all the differences between an Englishman and an American, that in politics is the strongest and the most essential. I cannot here, in one paragraph, define that difference with sufficient clearness to make my definition satisfactory. Still, the difference is apparent. The American and the Englishman are both *republicans.* The governments of the United States and of England are probably the two purest republican governments in the world. And yet no men can be much further apart in politics than the Englishman and the American. The American puts a ballot-box into the hands of every citizen, and takes his stand upon that and upon that only. It is the duty of an American citizen to vote, and when he has voted he need not trouble himself again until it is time to vote again. The Englishman, on the other hand, will have no ballot-box, and is by no means inclined to depend exclusively upon voters or upon voting. As far as voting can show it, he desires to get the sense of the country. The political action of the United States is undoubtedly the more logical and the clearer. That of England is, indeed, so illogical and so little clear that it would be impossible for any other nation to assume it. The political action of the United States might be *assumed* by any nation tomorrow, and all its strength and weakness might be carried across the sea in a few written rules, as are the *prescriptions* of a *physician.* With the English, political action has grown out of habit, has been fostered by tradition, has developed uncared for and perhaps in part unnoticed. It can be written in no book, can be described in no words, can be copied by no statesmen.

Exercises and Questions for Analysis

I

Define each of the following italicized words as used in the context of the sentence:

1. The American is not like an Englishman in his mind, in his *aspirations,* in his *tastes,* or in his politics.
2. In his mind he is less *indulgent* of *stupidity.*
3. He is more *brittle* and less *malleable.*
4. The mind of the American has more *incision.*
5. The French have won for themselves an international *reputation.*
6. I *acknowledged* the *rebuke.*
7. The American and the Englishman are both *republicans.*
8. The political action of the United States might be *assumed* by any nation tomorrow, and all its strength and weakness might be carried across the sea in a few written rules, as are the *prescriptions* of a *physician.*

II

Answer the following questions and write the assignment:

1. Point out the subject in the last two sentences of this selection. Point out the verb. Is there only one verb? Why?
2. Pick out and list all the compound sentences you can find; all the complex sentences; all the compound-complex sentences.

3. Analyze carefully the structure of the second sentence in the fourth paragraph.

III

Read the following statement closely and write the assignments:

1. Notice the methods of comparison and contrast used in this selection. There are three conventional ways of comparing or contrasting two or more things. 1. All the characteristics of the first thing may be stated in one paragraph and the second thing in the second paragraph. Then the characteristics of the first thing may be compared and contrasted with those of the second thing in a third paragraph. 2. All the characteristics of the first thing may be stated in a single paragraph. Then the characteristics of the second thing may be taken up one at a time and the comparison or contrast with the characteristics of the first thing may be made as each is taken up. 3. A single characteristic of the first thing is compared with a single characteristic of the second thing. Then each other characteristic of both things is taken up in turn.

   Assume that A and B are two things to be compared, each having five characteristics. The three methods then can be represented in the following way:

   1. Paragraph I–A 12345
      Paragraph II–B 12345
      Paragraph III–1(A-B), 2(A-B), 3(A-B), 4(A-B), 5(A-B)
   2. Paragraph I–A 12345
      Paragraph II–B1-A1, B2-A2, B3-A3, B4-A4, B5-A5
   3. Paragraph I–A1-B1, A2-B2, A3-B3, A4-B4, A5-B5

2. Are all three of these methods employed in this selection? Point out the section in the selection where each different method of comparison and contrast is employed.
3. Outline this selection in detail using the method and the style suggested on the preceding pages.
4. Write two different versions of the same incident. For example, you might try to describe something you have seen first as it really appeared to you, and then as you think it might have appeared to someone else. After you have written the two versions, then compare and contrast them.

SECTION VIII

Logic and Informal Argument

SLOAN WILSON

The Case against *Fraternities*

Last winter a student at the Massachusetts Institute of *Technology* was killed while being *initiated* into a *fraternity*. He had been left out in the woods alone on a cold night by his "brothers" and was trying to find his way back to his campus. While crossing a frozen *pond*, which he may have mistaken for a snow-covered *meadow* in the darkness, he fell through the ice and was drowned.

Fraternities are allowed a good deal of *latitude* in the name of good clean *horseplay*, but they aren't supposed to kill people. All sorts of reforms were undertaken on the MIT campus, and the paid executive secretaries of fraternities all around the country were kept busy writing statements about the good deeds their members have substituted for old-fashioned *hazing*.

In spite of this, the incident of the boy falling through the ice in the darkness dealt a hard blow to fraternities. A lot of people began to wonder what all these Greek-letters really mean and whether fraternities aren't fundamentally *vicious*.

I think this is too bad because there is nothing vicious about fraternities. They can be called stupid, witless, juvenile, and purposeless associations much like the "clubs" small boys organize in back-yard shacks, but they can't be called vicious. Most of

From *The American Weekly* (October 7, 1956). Reprinted by permission of the author.

them have a kind of Boy Scout code of honor which makes their members burst with pride.

It bothers me to see fraternities criticized for the wrong reasons. Fraternities can easily prove they're not vicious, and they can easily change their initiation procedures to avoid unfortunate fatal accidents. In doing this, they may seem to have undertaken important reforms, and to have justified their existence. That, of course, would be nonsense. The existence of fraternities can't be *justified* any more than can many other *manifestations* of *adolescence.*

Very few people seem to understand what fraternities (and sororities and other secret clubs) are. They are organizations of students which ask some people to be members and *exclude* others. The standards of acceptance are vague and are established by the fraternity members themselves.

The goal of each fraternity usually is to get as its members the "best" students enrolled in an institution of learning. By "best" I don't mean the most brilliant or the most moral, I mean "best" as construed by the adolescents themselves.

To some this means rich, handsome, and white Protestants, a definition which in its *guileless witlessness* almost achieves *innocence.* To others, "best" means those *possessed* of the *prevailing code of social behavior,* or the best available after "better" fraternities have taken their pick.

Fraternities like to boast about getting "a good cross-section" of students as members, but on almost any campus an old hand will be able to tell which fraternities specialize in attracting the local version of *socialites,* which ones pride themselves on varsity athletes, and which ones are havens for the boy intellectuals. There are fraternities especially known for heavy drinking, for wild parties, and for *luxurious* living.

On almost any campus it is easy to find which fraternities are for white Protestants only, which ones are largely Catholic, and which ones are largely Jewish. In the past, many fraternities *oafishly* placed written articles of racial or religious restriction in their constitutions. Recently there have been many hasty and *red-faced* attempts to bring the constitutions of fraternities into line with the constitution of the United States, but no one can seriously doubt that *intolerance* and *bigotry* is still practiced by many fraternities.

From campus to campus and from year to year the chapters of fraternities change, but each tends to seek students of like nature. On each campus there will be the "best" fraternity—the one which has attracted the most prosperous Protestant students of athletic, academic, or social distinction.

The "best" fraternity sometimes can make the superficially believable claim that it gets a cross-section of the "best" students. But there can be only one "best" fraternity. Many others are established to *assuage* the feelings of those who fail to get in the "best" fraternity. If the "ins" organize, so do the "outs." If students, for one of many reasons, are excluded from one fraternity, the *thin-skinned* ones frequently organize a fraternity of their own.

Thus every student is neatly *compartmented* on many an American campus, and the main purpose of a college education is, in a sense, defeated. That is the *irony* of fraternities; they do the most harm to their own members.

In the past many tears have been shed over the *plight* of students who aren't asked to join a fraternity. In my opinion these students are lucky. They may have momentarily hurt feelings and they may spend most of their college days feeling themselves to be *outcasts,* but they do not have the *stultifying* experience of *associating* only with people of their own kind for their entire college career.

They are not linked by false pride in having "made" an institution which was not worth making in the first place. They can, once their *wounded pride* is healed, become one with those very best college students of all: those who wouldn't think of joining a fraternity.

Today more and more students feel that their intelligence

is insulted when they are invited to participate in the *trick handclasps, juvenile insignia,* the *paddling of posteriors,* the abandonment of young boys in the woods at night, and all the rest of it.

For decades many American college students were *notorious* for their *immaturity,* but since the war they have shown signs of growing up. The really brilliant students nowadays are taking a hard look at the "advantages" fraternities pretend to offer and are recognizing them as childish frauds.

One of these "advantages" is "brotherhood," which is achieved by denying the fundamental brotherhood of all men, by excluding people of different *mien or manner.*

Mature students are realizing that they do not need Greek letters to have friendship. The *veterans* of World War II who returned to college found that they could drink beer without being "initiated," and they weren't *enthusiastic* about being paddled or taken on "*scary*" expeditions by *beardless youths.* Most of these ex-servicemen ignored fraternities. They have set a sensible example for their younger brothers and their sons.

Another so-called advantage of fraternities is the development of social ease, or "*savoir faire.*" Apparently a lot of *clods* who blushed at the thought of asking a woman to dance and who didn't know a *salad fork* from a *pitchfork* have, over the years, joined fraternities and found *enlightenment* in the field of *modes and manners.* Special classes for such poor souls could be provided—if fraternities should die of their own *clownishness.*

What other advantages do fraternities pretend to offer? A "sense of belonging" is one. Undoubtedly there are a few students on every campus who are afraid to stand up as individuals. For such people it is not enough to be a member of a family, a church, a college, a nation, and the human race. They like to believe they're something special, because they have achieved membership in an organization which keeps others out. Fortunately, most colleges now have *psychiatric clinics* for such students.

There is one other *"advantage"* which fraternities *dangle* before the eyes of *prospective* members, but even the fraternity members themselves are sometimes ashamed to boast of it. That is the "advantage" of "contacts" made at college who will later be useful in helping a fraternity member to get a job. It would seem that many of the "brothers" lack confidence in themselves and are afraid they will be unable to get a job as good as they deserve without outside aid.

Whatever the reason, fraternity members often show pathetic hope in, and dependence on, one another for help in earning a living. On what frail straws these poor souls lean!

I have been in the hiring business on several occasions, and I have been amazed at the eagerness of many fraternity "brothers" to *blackball* one another. On many occasions people have said to me something like this: "Jim Jones! He was a member of my fraternity in college, and I knew him well. He's a bum—a real bum!"

In the business world, the accuracy of the recommendations a man gives others greatly affects his own reputation, and no old-school-tie sentiment affects the judgment given by capable and ambitious men. I suppose some jobs are reserved for *down-and-outers* by their fraternity brothers, but, fortunately, government relief programs are relieving fraternities of these responsibilities.

In any case, really capable students don't spend their days on the campus worrying about "contacts" for jobs after graduation.

No really brilliant student who is mature and psychologically whole could possibly become a member of a fraternity nowadays, any more than he could join the *Ku Klux Klan,* or one of those clubs whose only requirement for membership is the mailing of a *cereal box top.* It probably would be wise for teachers and parents to point this out to the boys and girls of college age who are not bright enough to perceive it for themselves.

But let's not exaggerate the evils of fraternities. There is nothing vicious about the boys and girls who join such organizations. Even those initiation stunts which result in fatal accidents, like the one last winter at MIT, are not the product of evil thinking. They are the result of not thinking at all.

Exercises and Questions for Analysis

I

Define each of the following italicized words as used in the context of the sentence. Each phrase in brackets should be defined as a unit:

1. Last winter a student at the Massachusetts Institute of *Technology* was killed while being *initiated* into a *fraternity.*
2. He may have mistaken a frozen *pond* for a snow-covered *meadow.*
3. Fraternities are allowed a good deal of *latitude* in the name of good clean *horseplay.*
4. Good deeds have been substituted for old-fashioned *hazing.*
5. Fraternities aren't fundamentally *vicious.*
6. The existence of fraternities can't be *justified* any more than can many other *manifestations* of *adolescence.*
7. They are organizations of students which ask some people to join and *exclude* others.
8. This is a definition which in its *guileless witlessness* almost achieves *innocence.*
9. "Best" means those *possessed* of the [*prevailing code of social behavior*].
10. There are those which specialize in attracting the local versions of *socialites.*
11. Some are known for *luxurious* living.
12. Many fraternities *oafishly* included articles of racial or religious restriction.
13. There have been many *red-faced* attempts to correct this.

14. *Intolerance* and *bigotry* is still practiced by many fraternities.
15. Many fraternities are established to *assuage* the feelings of students who are not admitted to the "best" fraternities.
16. *Thin-skinned* students frequently organize their own groups.
17. Every student is neatly *compartmented.*
18. That is the *irony* of fraternities.
19. Tears have been shed over the *plight* of some students.
20. They may feel themselves to be *outcasts.*
21. They do not have the *stultifying* experience of *associating* only with people of their own kind.
22. Their [*wounded pride*] will heal.
23. Many students do not want to participate in the [*trick handclasps*], [*juvenile insignia*], and the [*paddling of posteriors*].
24. American college students were *notorious* for their *immaturity.*
25. Some fraternities exclude people of different [*mien or manner*].
26. The *veterans* of World War II weren't *enthusiastic* about being taken on "*scary*" expeditions by [*beardless youths*].
27. Another advantage of fraternities is the development of ["*savoir faire*"].
28. A lot of *clods* didn't know a [*salad fork*] from a *pitchfork.*
29. They found *enlightenment* in the field of [*modes and manners*].
30. Fraternities may die of their own *clownishness.*
31. Most colleges have [*psychiatric clinics*].
32. Fraternities *dangle advantages* before the eyes of *prospective* members.
33. Fraternity brothers are anxious to *blackball* one another.
34. Some jobs are reserved for [*down-and-outers*].
35. Students are not apt to join the [*Ku Klux Klan*] or a club whose only requirement for membership is the mailing of a [*cereal box top*].

II

Answer the following questions:

1. Pick out all the compound, complex, and compound-complex sentences you can find. Compare the numbers with the num-

bers found in the selection "The Englishman and the American" by Anthony Trollope. What generalizations can you make about the style of the two writers on the basis of this comparison? In your discussion be sure to include the matter of the audience.

2. Analyze the verb sequence in the first paragraph, in the fifteenth paragraph.

III

Read the following statements closely. Then answer the questions:

1. This selection is obviously an argument. Exactly what is an argument? Does this selection meet the requirements of that form? Does it succeed or fail? In what ways does it succeed or fail?
2. Examine carefully the logic of the author's argument. Does he commit logical errors? Are they intentional? Identify as many of the errors in logic as you can find. Label them. What sorts of logical errors seem to be most common? Can this selection be considered to be propagandistic? Why?
3. Throughout the selection the writer puts certain words in quotation marks. What is his purpose? Is it effective?

HERBERT L. BROWN

The Case for Fraternities

To prove how vicious college fraternities are, Mr. Sloan Wilson last week used as his primary example a fraternity initiation at MIT in which a *pledge* fell through the ice and was drowned in a pond.

I am sure that on *sober second thought* Mr. Wilson will agree that he has not proved fraternities "stupid," "witless," "juvenile," and "purposeless" (or any of the other angry adjectives he hurled at them), by his single example of tragedy. He should be well aware that several hundred thousand college students are prevented from falling into holes by fraternities—from falling into social awkwardness, failing grades, *athletic inertia,* and ignorance of group living.

I refuse to reply to Mr. Wilson in the style of his attack; rather I will answer his "arguments" with a defense of fraternities, which I will attempt to make more well-proportioned and *level-headed* than his *broadside.*

What would Mr. Wilson find if he would look for the truth about college fraternities? He would find, first of all, that there are 12,000 chapters of Greek-letter societies in the United States with a total membership of four million. If fraternities are "purposeless," why have 225,000 new members joined them in the past three years? If fraternities are "unnecessary," why have 381 new chapters been established in the same period? Would so

From *The American Weekly* (October 14, 1956). Reprinted by permission of *The American Weekly.*

many young Americans in so many places go into organizations that are "stupid, witless, and juvenile"?

If Mr. Wilson believes so, then his faith in the wisdom of the American people is pretty weak. Fraternity life is continuing to *flourish* because fraternities exist to answer genuine student and college needs, because fraternities help in the attainment of worthy educational, social, and personal goals.

"On our campus," says Chancellor Ethan A. H. Shepley of Washington University (St. Louis), "fraternities are a very real asset. I frankly don't know what we would do without their influence and support. We are proud of them and the record they have made." The *testimony* of dozens of other college presidents—men like George Bowman of Kent State (Ohio), Harlan Hatcher of Michigan, and Milton Eisenhower of Johns Hopkins University—*tells the same story:* fraternities are needed.

The reason that the great good in fraternities is so clouded is that, unfortunately, only the *freak prank* makes the *headlines;* only the tragic *slip* arouses righteous *indignation.* The many valuable things that American fraternities do for their members, their colleges, and their communities—their many fine purposes and achievements—go *unheralded* because activities like working in a community chest drive, or teaching a student how to conduct himself socially, are hardly the stuff for news.

When a student is accidently hurt in what is usually harmless fun, people are quick to cry out that fraternities should be *driven from the land like the plague.* But when a student's marks are raised by the help he receives from his fraternity brothers, when a community Red Cross receives blood from a chapter, when a college is saved from a housing problem by a group with Greek letters, too few people know about it.

Exactly what are the values of American fraternities—to the students, to the school, and to the college community—values that are so often lost behind *scare headlines* and distorted by attacks like Mr. Wilson's?

Fraternities make important contributions to the minds, personalities, and characters of their members.

First, each fraternity has a tutoring system in which members proficient in certain studies help members who are less proficient. It is often the coaching of a fraternity brother that prevents a fraternity man from failing a course.

Mr. Wilson mocks a fraternity's "boy scout code of honor which makes their members fairly burst with pride," but one great source of fraternity pride is the achievement of high scholastic marks by its members. Fraternity brothers do not tutor one another simply to prevent failure in subjects. They exchange knowledge so that the students in their chapter can make the best marks on the campus.

Ask any fraternity man and he will tell you how often a "*seminar*" with his brothers the night before an exam raised his mark. If this is a "boy scout" code, then to be out of the "boy scouts" is to enjoy being a *moron.*

It is an undisputed fact that the social programs of fraternities give members *poise* and polish which would develop more slowly —and perhaps not at all—if the students were to live alone. Fraternity parties, outings, dances, and sports *enable* a student to *shed* his *adolescent awkwardness* and learn to move with confidence among members of his own and the opposite sex. In addition to helping a man's grades, fraternities help him feel at ease on a dance floor, on the baseball diamond, on a committee—or any facet of group living.

Fraternities develop qualities of leadership in their members. They *inculcate* in them standards of good *conduct,* good *manners,* good *taste,* and good *sportsmanship.* Most important, fraternities teach members to live together in harmony and understanding.

Mr. Wilson rejoices over the advantage a college student receives when he does *not* join a fraternity. Shortly after graduation, most of these students will be asked—with no refusal permitted—to join a larger and less friendly fraternity called the United States Army.

Who does Mr. Wilson think will be better prepared to *cope* with the trials of group living found in military service—the "*lone wolf*" or the fraternity man? The essence of America, as President Eisenhower has so often said, is the team—both in peace and war.

And does Mr. Wilson believe that the "lone wolf" can learn the principles of self-government in his single room? He can read about them in history textbooks; but the fraternity man works with and studies these principles as they are alive in the political organization of his chapter.

Critics like Mr. Wilson are silent about the *financial aid* that *Greek-letter societies* constantly provide for students. Through the years, many fraternities have built up foundations to enable needier members to continue higher education. Without grants from these foundations, many boys would never get a college education.

How do fraternities help the college? First, and most important, they do so by housing many students. Fraternities furnish high-quality housing facilities which many colleges could never offer. If Mr. Wilson considers this "juvenile," then we must assume that he considers it "adult" for college students to live in tents.

Lest Mr. Wilson think that the only activity of college fraternities is sending students out to fall through icy ponds, here are others that might interest him:

Fraternities throughout America donate blood, work with community chest drives, give children's Christmas parties, entertain orphans and underprivileged children. They operate foreign student exchange programs, sell Easter and Christmas seals, collect clothing for refugees. They raise funds for the fight against polio, cerebral palsy, heart disease, and cancer; assist in the *Care* program; and in many other ways help local, American, and world society.

Such activities are typical of fraternities, which Mr. Wilson considers "stupid and purposeless." He and other critics continue to shout: "Yes, but what about *'hell week'* and discrimination."

All right, what about them? The people making the most noise about an occasional "hell week" abuse do not seem to hear—or care—that fraternities themselves are *eliminating archaic hazing* practices. And no segment of American society has been more shocked or distressed over "hell week" tragedies than the college men and women of Greek-letter societies.

Fraternity members are the first to admit that outmoded hazing practices are a shortcoming in the fraternity system. In the past ten years, "hell week" has become "help week" on most campuses. Instead of getting lost in the woods, students now spend this *initiation* period working on chores which improve their fraternity houses, their school, and their community.

Fraternities have been further condemned for being selective in choosing their members, but can you, Mr. Wilson, name a single social organization in this country that does not practice some type of *selectivity* in the choice of its members? But just to set the record straight, a few decades ago forty-four of the fifty-eight social fraternities in the National Interfraternity Conference at that time had restrictive membership clauses based on race, color, or national origin in their constitutions. Today, no more than a dozen of the sixty-one groups in the Conference have such clauses.

People are innate joiners, Mr. Wilson. If there were no fraternities at colleges, *cliques* of people with similar interests would, naturally, get together anyway.

In fact, consider what colleges would be *without* fraternities.

There would be fewer students (for there would be fewer scholarships), lower marks, overcrowded dormitories, and less effective social, athletic, and self government programs for great numbers of students.

Fraternities—or groups like them (whether they are called "eating clubs" or "houses" or "societies")—will always exist at colleges because they answer a definite need. Dr. Milton Eisenhower—who has been president of three colleges and who was recently appointed by his brother Dwight to help make North, Central, and South America into one big fraternity—summed it up this way: "Fraternities and sororities are workshops in understanding and cooperation. They are *anvils* upon which the character of individuals may be *fashioned* for *service beyond self.*"

Exercises and Questions for Analysis

I

Define each of the following italicized words as used in the context of the sentence. Each phrase in brackets should be defined as a unit:

1. A *pledge* fell through the ice and was drowned.
2. On [*sober second thought*] Mr. Wilson will agree with me.
3. College students are kept from falling into [*athletic inertia*] by fraternities.
4. I will attempt to make my answer more *level-headed* than Mr. Wilson's *broadside*.
5. Fraternity life is continuing to *flourish.*
6. The *testimony* of other college presidents [*tells the same story*].
7. Only the [*freak pranks*] make the *headlines,* only the tragic *slip* arouses *indignation.*
8. Many valuable things go *unheralded.*
9. Fraternities should be [*driven from the land like the plague*].
10. Values are often lost behind [*scare headlines*].
11. Often a "*seminar*" has helped to raise a student's grades.

12. To be out of the boy scouts is to enjoy being a *moron.*
13. The social programs of fraternities give the members *poise.*
14. Fraternity activities *enable* a student to *shed* his [*adolescent awkwardness*].
15. Fraternities *inculcate* in their members standards of good *conduct,* good *manners,* good *taste,* and good *sportsmanship.*
16. Does Mr. Wilson think the [*"lone wolf"*] or the fraternity man will be better able to *cope* with problems of group living?
17. [*Greek-letter societies*] offer [*financial aid*] to students.
18. What about [*"hell week"*]?
19. Fraternities are *eliminating archaic hazing* practices.
20. Students now spend this *initiation* period doing useful work.
21. Every organization practices some sort of *selectivity* in the choice of its members.
22. *Cliques* of people with similar interests would naturally get together.
23. Fraternities are *anvils* upon which the character of individuals may be *fashioned* for [*service beyond self*].

II

Answer the following questions:

1. Analyze the last sentence in the fourteenth paragraph. Does it contain an error? If so, identify the error and correct it.
2. A semicolon is used in the second sentence in the eighteenth paragraph. Is this usage correct? What might be better?
3. Analyze the single sentence which constitutes the twenty-first paragraph. What kind of verb is used? Can the sentence be improved?

III

Read the following statements carefully, answer the questions, and write the assignment:

1. Examine the logic of this essay carefully. Look particularly at the third, fourth, sixteenth, twentieth, and twenty-sixth paragraphs. Can you detect any errors in logic? Are these errors intentional or accidental? What is the danger of such logical errors in an argument?

2. Is this essay an effective argument? In what ways does it succeed or fail as argument? Do the errors in logic mentioned above contribute to the essay's effectiveness? Does this argument adequately answer the previous selection, *The Case against Fraternities*?
3. Again, as in the previous selection, the writer puts certain words in quotation marks. Is his purpose consistently the same as that of Mr. Wilson? What do these quoted words contribute to the selection?
4. At the beginning of the selection, Mr. Brown writes, "I refuse to reply to Mr. Wilson in the style of his attack; rather I will answer his 'arguments' with a defense of fraternities, which I will attempt to make more well-proportioned and level-headed than his broadside." What is the effect of this statement? Does Mr. Brown keep the promise implied in this statement? In what ways does he either keep or violate this implied promise?
5. Write a case for and against any one of the following: coeducation, freedom of the press, universal suffrage, democracy, compulsory education.

SECTION IX

Formal Argument

HERMAN WOUK

A Talk on Advertising

Marquis, while you were talking I looked around this table and saw that [nearly] everyone here wins *subsistence* through the activity called *advertising*. Now, I realize that you invited me in the absence, enforced by your sedentary ways, of *stuffed tiger heads* or other *trophies* on your walls, a live artist being the *equivalent* of a dead beast as a *social ornament*. I will not question your motive because it has given me a chance to do a beautiful and good thing. I should like to *entreat* all these gentlemen to *redeem* the strange, *bittersweet miracle* of their lives, while there is yet time, by giving up the advertising business at once.

Has it ever occurred to any of you gentlemen to examine the peculiar fact that you find bread in your mouths daily? How does this happen? Who is it that you have persuaded to feed you? The obvious answer is that you buy your food, but this just states the question in another, less clear way, because money is nothing but an *exchange token*. Drop the confusing element of money from the whole process, and the question I've *posed* must *confront* you *bleakly*. What is it that you do, that entitles you to eat?

A shoemaker gives shoes for his bread. Well. A singer sings for her supper. Well. A capitalist leads a large enterprise. Well. A pilot flies, a coal-miner digs, a sailor moves things, a minis-

From *Aurora Dawn* (1947). Copyright permission granted by Harold Matson Company.

ter preaches, an author tells stories, a laundryman washes, an auto worker makes cars, a painter makes pictures, a street car conductor moves people, a stenographer writes down words, a *lumberjack* saws, and a tailor sews. The people with the *victuals* appreciate these services and cheerfully feed the performers. But what does an advertising man do?

He *induces* human beings to want things they don't want.

Now, I will be deeply obliged if you will tell me by what links of logic anybody can be convinced that your activity—the creation of want where want does not exist—is a useful one and should be rewarded with food. Doesn't it seem, rather, the worst sort of *mischief*, deserving to be *starved* into *extinction*?

None of you, however, is anything but well fed; yet I am sure that until this moment it has never occurred to you on what a *dubious* basis your *feeding* is *accomplished*. I shall tell you exactly how you eat. You induce people to use more things than they naturally desire—the more useless and undesirable the article, the greater the advertising effort needed to *dispose* of it, —and in all the profit from that unnatural purchasing, you share. You are fed by the makers of undesired things, who exchange these things for food by means of your arts and give you your *share of the haul.*

Lest you think I *oversimplify*, I give you an *obvious illustration.* People naturally crave meat; so the advertising of meat is on a *negligible* scale. However, nobody is born *craving* tobacco, and even its slaves *instinctively loathe* it. So the advertising of tobacco is the largest item of expense in its distribution. It follows, of course, that advertising men thrive most richly in the service of utterly useless commodities like tobacco or *under-arm-pastes*, or in a field where there is a hopeless *plethora* of *goods*, such as soap or whiskey.

But the great evil of advertising is not that it is unproductive and wasteful; were it so, it would be no worse than idleness. No. Advertising *blasts* everything that is good and beautiful in this land with a *horrid* spreading *mildew.* It has *tarnished Creation.* What is sweet to any of you in the world? Love? Nature? Art? Language? Youth? Behold them all, yoked by advertising in the harness of commerce!

Aurora Dawn! Has any of you enough of an ear for English to realize what a crime against the language is in that [trade] name? Aurora *is* the dawn! The *redundancy* should *assail* your ears like the *shriek* of a bad *hinge.* But you are so *numbed* by *habit* that it conveys no offense. So it is with all your *barbarities.* Shakespeare used the *rhyming* of "double" and "bubble" to *create* two *immortal* lines in *Macbeth.* You use it to help sell your Dubl-Bubl Shampoo, and you have no slightest sense of doing anything wrong. Should someone tell you that language is the *Promethean fire* that lifts man above the animals and that you are smothering the flame in mud, you would stare. You are staring. Let me tell you without images, then, that you are cheapening speech until it is ceasing to be an honest method of exchange, and that the people, not knowing that the English in a radio commercial is meant to be a lie and the English in the President's speech which follows, a truth, will in the end fall into a *paralyzing skepticism* in which all *utterances* will be *disbelieved.*

God made a great green wonderland when He spread out the span of the United States. Where is the square mile inhabited by men wherein advertising has not *drowned out the land's meek hymn* with the *blare of billboards?* By what right do you turn Nature into a *painted hag* crying "Come, buy"?

A few heavenly talents brighten the world in each generation. Artistic *inspiration* is *entrusted* to weak human beings who can be tempted with gold. Has advertising *scrupled* to buy up the *holiest* of these gifts and set them to work *peddling?*

And the traffic in lovely youth! By the lord, gentlemen, I would close every advertising *agency* in the country tomorrow, if only to head off the *droves* of silly girls, *sufficiently* cursed with beauty, who troop into the cities each month, most of them to be *stained and scarred,* a few to find *ashy* success in the *hardening* life of a *model!* When will a strong voice call a halt to this *dismal pilgrimage,* this *Children's Crusade to the Unholy Land?* When will someone *denounce* the *snaring allurements* of the *picture magazines?* When will someone tell these babies that for each girl who grins on a magazine cover a hundred weep in back rooms, and that even the grin is a bought and forced thing that fades with the flash of the photographer's bulb, leaving a face grim with scheming or heartbreak?

To what end is all this lying, *vandalism,* and misuse? You are trying to Sell; never mind what, never mind how, never mind to whom—just Sell, Sell, Sell! Small wonder that in good old American slang "sell" means *"fraud"!* Come now! Do you hesitate to promise *requited* love to miserable girls, triumph to failures, *virility* to *weaklings,* even *prowess* to little children, for the price of a mouth wash or a breakfast food? Does it ever occur to you to be ashamed to live by *preying* on the *myriad* little tragedies of *unfulfillment* which make your methods pay so well?

I trust that I am offending everybody very deeply. An artist has the privileges of the court fool, you know. I paint because I see with a seeing eye, an eye that familiarity never glazes. Advertising strikes me as it would a man from Mars and as it undoubtedly appears to the angels: an occupation the aim of which is *subtle prevarication* for *gain,* and the effect of which is the *blighting* of everything fair and pleasant in our time with the *garish fungus* of *greed.* If I have made all of you, or just one of you, repent of this career and determine to seek decent work, I will not have breathed in vain today.

Exercises and Questions for Analysis

I

Define each of the following italicized words as used in the context of the sentence. Each phrase in brackets should be defined as a unit:

1. Everyone here wins *subsistence* through the activity called *advertising.*
2. You invite me in the absence of [*stuffed tiger heads*] or other *trophies.*
3. A live artist is the *equivalent* of a dead beast as a [*social ornament*].
4. I should like to *entreat* all these gentlemen to *redeem* the strange, *bittersweet miracle* of their lives.
5. Money is nothing but an [*exchange token*].
6. The question I've *posed* must *confront* you *bleakly.*
7. A *lumberjack* saws.
8. The people with the *victuals* appreciate these services.
9. An advertising man *induces* people to want things they don't want.
10. Doesn't it seem the worst sort of *mischief,* deserving to be *starved* into *extinction?*
11. Has it ever occurred to you on what a *dubious* basis your *feeding* is *accomplished?*
12. The more useless the article, the greater the advertising effort needed to *dispose* of it.
13. They give you your [*share of the haul*].
14. *Lest* you think I *oversimplify,* I give you an [*obvious illustration*].
15. The advertising of meat is on a *negligible* scale.
16. Nobody is born *craving* tobacco, and even its slaves *instinctively loathe* it.
17. Advertising men thrive in the service of *under-arm-pastes,* or in a field where there is a *plethora* of *goods.*

18. Advertising *blasts* everything that is good and beautiful in this land with a *horrid* spreading *mildew.*

19. It has *tarnished Creation.*

20. The *redundancy* should *assail* your ears like the *shriek* of a bad *hinge.*

21. You are *numbed* by *habit.*

22. So it is with all your *barbarities.*

23. Shakespeare used the *rhyming* of "double" and "bubble" to *create* two *immortal* lines in *Macbeth.*

24. Language is the [*Promethean fire*] that lifts man above the animals.

25. The people will in the end fall into a [*paralyzing skepticism*] in which all *utterance* will be *disbelieved.*

26. Where is the square mile inhabited by men wherein advertising has not [*drowned out*] [*the land's meek hymn*] with [*the blare of billboards*]?

27. Nature is a [*painted hag*] crying "Come, buy!"

28. Artistic *inspiration* is *entrusted* to weak human beings.

29. Advertising has not *scrupled* to buy up the *holiest* of these gifts and set them to work *peddling.*

30. I would close every advertising *agency* in the country tomorrow, if only to head off the *droves* of silly girls, *sufficiently* cursed with beauty, who troop into the cities each month, most of them to be [*stained and scarred*], a few to find *ashy* success in the *hardening* life of a *model.*

31. When will a strong voice call a halt to this *dismal pilgrimage,* this [*Children's Crusade to the Unholy Land*]?

32. When will someone *denounce* the [*snaring allurements*] of the [*picture magazines*]?

33. To what end is all this *vandalism?*

34. In American slang "sell" means "*fraud.*"

35. Do you hesitate to promise *requited* love to miserable girls, triumph to failures, *virility* to *weaklings,* even *prowess* to little children.

36. Does it ever occur to you to be ashamed to live by *preying* on the *myriad* little tragedies of *unfulfillment?*

37. The aim of advertising is *subtle prevarication* for *gain.*
38. The effect of advertising is the *blighting* of everything fair and pleasant in our time with the *garish fungus* of *greed.*

II

Answer the following questions:

1. The third paragraph is composed largely of one long sentence. Should this sentence be broken up into several sentences? Could it be punctuated differently?
2. Examine carefully the structure of the eighth paragraph. Is "No." a sentence? Are the following sentences: "Love? Nature? Art? Language? Youth?" Why are these words written as they are?

III

Read the following statements and questions closely. Then answer the questions:

1. Unlike most of the other selections which you have read, this piece of writing was intended to be a speech. How do you know? What devices clearly indicate that it was intended to be spoken? How does it differ from other selections?
2. Why can this selection be included under the heading "Formal Argument," while the two previous ones are listed under the heading "Informal Argument and Logic"? What are the differences between the level of this argument and the level of the two previous ones? What other differences exist between these selections?
3. Since this selection is obviously an argument, what is its purpose? Is it an effective argument? In what ways is it effective or ineffective?
4. Can you detect any logical fallacies in the author's argument? If so, what are they? Where do they occur? Are they intentional or accidental? Do they contribute to, or detract from, the effectiveness of the author's purpose?

ALEXIS DE TOCQUEVILLE

Universal Suffrage Does Not Guarantee Wise Leadership

In Europe we are *at a loss* how to judge the true character and the permanent *instincts* of democracy. In America the people *reign* without *impediment,* and they have no perils to dread and no injuries to avenge. In America democracy is given up to its own *propensities;* its course is natural and its activity is unrestrained; there, consequently, its real character must be judged.

Universal suffrage has been adopted in all the states of the Union; it consequently exists in communities which occupy very different positions in the social scale. I have had opportunities of observing its effects in different localities and amongst races of men who are nearly strangers to each other in their language, their religion, and their modes of life; in Louisiana as well as in New England, in Georgia as well as in Canada. I have remarked that universal suffrage is far from producing in America either all the good or all the evil consequences which may be expected from it in Europe, and that its effects generally differ very much from those which are attributed to it.

Many people in Europe are apt to believe without saying it, or to say without believing it, that one of the great advantages

From *Democracy in America* (1835-39).

of universal suffrage is that it *entrusts* the direction of affairs to men who are worthy of the public confidence. They admit that the people are unable to govern of themselves, but they *aver* that the people always wish the welfare of the state and *instinctively designate* those who are animated by the same good wishes and who are the most fit to *wield* the *supreme* authority. I confess that the observations I made in America by no means *coincide* with these opinions. On my arrival in the United States I was surprised to find so much distinguished talent among the subjects and so little among the heads of government. It is a constant fact that at the present day the ablest men in the United States are rarely placed at the head of affairs. It must be acknowledged that such has been the result in proportion as democracy has outstepped all its former limits. The race of American *statesmen* has evidently *dwindled* most remarkably in the course of the last fifty years.

Several causes may be assigned for this *phenomenon.* It is impossible, after the most *strenuous exertions,* to raise the intelligence of the people above a certain level. Whatever may be the *facilities* of acquiring information, whatever may be the *profusion* of easy methods and cheap science, the human mind can never be instructed and developed without devoting considerable time to these objects.

The greater or the less possibility of subsisting without labor is therefore the necessary boundary of intellectual improvement. This boundary is more remote in some countries and more restricted in others, but it must exist somewhere as long as the people are *constrained* to work in order to procure the means of *subsistence;* that is to say, as long as they continue to be the people. It is therefore quite as difficult to imagine a state in which all the citizens should be very well informed as a state in which they should all be wealthy. These two difficulties are *correlative.* I readily admit that the mass of the citizens sincerely wish to promote the welfare of the country. I even allow that the lower classes mix fewer considerations of personal interest with their patriotism than the higher orders. It is, however, always more or less difficult for them to *discern* the best means of attaining the end which they sincerely desire. Long and patient observation and much acquired knowledge are *requisite* to form a just estimate of the character of a single individual. Men of the greatest genius often fail to do it. Can it then be supposed that the common people will always succeed? The people have neither the time nor the means for an investigation of this kind. Their conclusions are hastily formed from a superficial inspection of the more prominent features of a question. Hence it often happens that fakes of all sorts are able to please the people, while their truest friends frequently fail to gain their confidence.

Moreover, the people not only lack that soundness of judgment which is necessary to select men really deserving of their confidence, but often have not the desire or the *inclination* to find them out. It cannot be denied that democratic institutions strongly tend to promote the feeling of envy in the human heart; not so much because they afford to everyone the means of rising to the same level with others as because those means perpetually disappoint the persons who employ them. Democratic institutions awaken and foster a passion for equality which they can never entirely satisfy. This complete equality eludes the grasp of the people at the very moment when they think they have grasped it, and "flies," as Pascal says, "with an eternal flight." The people are excited in the pursuit of an advantage which is more precious because it is not sufficiently remote to be unknown or sufficiently near to be enjoyed. The lower orders are *agitated* by the chance of success. They are irritated by its uncertainty. And they pass from the enthusiasm of pursuit to the exhaustion of ill success, and finally to the *acrimony* of disappointment. Whatever *transcends* their own limits appears to be an *obstacle* to their desires. There is no superiority, however legitimate it may be, which is not irksome in their sight.

In the United States the people do not hate the higher classes of society, but they are not favorably inclined towards them and carefully exclude them from the exercise of authority. They do not dread distinguished talents, but they are rarely fond of them. In general, everyone who rises without the aid of the people seldom obtains their favor.

While the natural *instincts* of democracy *induce* the people to reject distinguished citizens as their rulers, an instinct not less strong induces able men to retire from *the political arena,* in which it is so difficult to retain their independence, or to advance without becoming *servile.* This opinion has been *candidly* expressed by at least one writer, who says, in speaking with high praise of that part of the Constitution which *empowers* the *executive* to *nominate* the judges: "It is indeed probable that the men who are best fitted to *discharge* the duties of this high office would have too much *reserve* in their manners, and too much *austerity* in their principles, for them to be returned by the majority at an election where universal suffrage is adopted." Such were the opinions which were printed without *contradiction* in America.

I hold it to be sufficiently demonstrated that universal suffrage is by no means a guarantee of the wisdom of the popular choice. Whatever its advantages may be, this is not one of them.

When serious dangers threaten the state, the people frequently succeed in selecting the citizens who are the most able to save it. It has been observed that man rarely retains his customary level in very critical circumstances; he rises above or sinks below his usual condition. The same thing is true of nations. Extreme perils sometimes quench the energy of a people instead of stimulating it. Such perils excite the energy of a people without directing their passions. Instead of clearing the perception of the people, these problems confuse their powers of perception. The Jews fought and killed each other amid the smoking ruins of their temple. But it is more common, both with nations and with individuals, to find extraordinary *virtues* developed from the very *imminence* of the danger. Great characters are then brought into relief, as the *edifices* which are usually concealed by the gloom of night are *illuminated* by the glare of a *conflagration.* At those dangerous times genius no longer hesitates to come forward; and the people, alarmed by the perils of their situation, bury their envious passions in oblivion. Great names may then be drawn from the urn of election.

I have already observed that the American statesmen of the present day are very inferior to those who stood at the head of affairs fifty years ago. This is as much a consequence of the circumstances as it is of the laws of the country. When America was struggling in the high cause of independence to *throw off the yoke* of another country, and when it was about to usher a new nation into the world, the spirits of its inhabitants were roused to the height which their great objects required. In this general excitement distinguished men were ready to anticipate the call of the community, and the people clung to them for support and placed them at the head of the government. But such events are rare. It is from the ordinary course of affairs that our judgment must be formed.

Exercises and Questions for Analysis

I

Define each of the following italicized words as used in the context of the sentence. Each phrase in brackets should be defined as a unit:

1. We are [*at a loss*] how to judge the permanent *instincts* of democracy.
2. The people *reign* without *impediment.*
3. Democracy is given up to its own *propensities.*
4. [*Universal suffrage*] has been adopted in all the states.
5. It *entrusts* the direction of affairs to worthy men.

6. They *aver* that the people *instinctively designate* those who are most fit to *wield* the *supreme* authority.
7. My observations do not *coincide* with these opinions.
8. The race of American *statesmen* has *dwindled.*
9. There are several causes for this *phenomenon.*
10. It is impossible, after the most *strenuous exertions,* to raise the intelligence of the people.
11. What are the *facilities* of acquiring information?
12. There is a *profusion* of easy methods.
13. The boundary must exist somewhere as long as the people are *constrained* to work in order to produce the means of *subsistence.*
14. These two difficulties are *correlative.*
15. It is always difficult to *discern* the best means.
16. Much acquired knowledge is *requisite* to form a just estimate.
17. The people do not have the *inclination* to find out.
18. The people are *agitated* by the chance of success.
19. They pass finally to the *acrimony* of disappointment.
20. Whatever *transcends* their own limits appears to be an *obstacle.*
21. The *instincts* of democracy *induce* the people to reject good leaders.
22. Another instinct induces able men to retire from [*the political arena*].
23. It is difficult to advance without becoming *servile.*
24. This opinion has been *candidly* expressed.
25. The Constitution *empowers* the *executive* to *nominate* judges.
26. Men who are fitted to *discharge* the duties of this office have too much *reserve* in their manners and too much *austerity* in their principles to be elected.
27. These opinions were printed without *contradiction.*
28. Extraordinary *virtues* often develop from the very *imminence* of danger.
29. *Edifices* may be *illuminated* by the glare of a *conflagration.*
30. America was struggling to [*throw off the yoke*] of another country.

II

Answer the following questions:

1. What is the subject of the second paragraph? How do you know?
2. Analyze the first sentence in the third paragraph. What is the referent for the first two "its" in this sentence? What is the function of the third "it"?
3. There is a semicolon in the second sentence at the top of page 116. Is this punctuation correct? Compare this sentence with the second sentence in the second paragraph on page 98.

III

Read the following questions slowly, answer them, and write the assignments:

1. How does this argument differ from the ones concerning fraternities?
2. Is this argument logical? What makes it either logical or illogical? What basic assumptions is the writer making?
3. Write a brief summary of the specific points of attack in this argument.
4. Write a detailed outline of this essay, making clear and specific distinctions between the material which is essential to the structure and the various comparisons and illustrations which merely support the structure.
5. Write a paper in which you either attack or defend the position taken by the author of this selection. Be sure that you take into account *all* of the major points of his argument, but at the same time avoid borrowing from him any of his illustrations.

Review

I. Vocabulary

Define each of the following words in a complete sentence. Then use each of the words in a sentence of your own.

1. frank
2. vented
3. wishbone
4. proclaimed
5. rawboned
6. maxims
7. harsh
8. rebuke
9. prescription
10. throne
11. awry
12. throng
13. portended
14. discipline
15. monarch
16. fancy
17. profligate
18. entrusts
19. faint
20. sallow
21. swore
22. brittle
23. reflection
24. malleable
25. frugal
26. exquisite
27. focus
28. musing
29. timid
30. incision

II. Special Terminology

Define each of the following:

1. comparison
2. analysis
3. contrast
4. argument

Distinguish between:

1. analysis and argument
2. character and characterization
3. cause and effect and comparison and contrast

III. Identification

In a few words, identify the following:

1. William H. Herndon
2. Walter Pater
3. Anthony Trollope
4. Nero
5. Sloan Wilson
6. Queen Elizabeth
7. Leonardo da Vinci
8. Cicero
9. Joseph Addison
10. Herman Wouk

IV. Content

Briefly answer the following questions:

1. What are the principal differences (in Trollope's opinion) between an Englishman and an American?
2. In general terms describe the painting called *Mona Lisa.*
3. What was the difference between the "Golden Age" of Rome and the age of iron which had preceded it?
4. According to de Tocqueville what is wrong with universal suffrage?
5. What does Herman Wouk think is wrong with advertising?

V. Composition

Write a paper in which you state in detail what you have learned from the second section of this book. Include such items as vocabulary, style, grammar, organization, and paragraphing, as well as factual material from the contents of the selection.

VI. Outline

Outline the last selection in this book.

APPENDIX

A Brief History of the English Language

English as a distinct language began to be spoken around the seventh century A.D. It was a highly-inflected Germanic language called Anglo-Saxon. Although words from other languages were added during subsequent raids and invasions, Anglo-Saxon remained essentially unchanged until the Norman invasion in 1066 A.D. After the Norman conquest, French became the official language of the country until approximately 1200. About this time a modified Anglo-Saxon, stripped of most of its inflected endings and heavily influenced by French, emerged as the dominant language which is now described as Middle English. It reached its greatest literary development with the English poet Geoffrey Chaucer, who lived from approximately 1340 to 1400. Under Renaissance influence, when increased interest in antiquity led to the introduction of many Latinate words, Middle English evolved into early New English. The possibilities of the language were enlarged by such great Renaissance poets as Spenser and Shakespeare, by such notable eighteenth-century prose writers as Dryden, Addison, Steele, Johnson, and by such modern novelists as Thackeray, Dickens, and Eliot. Thus English has con-

Indo-European Languages

(c. 3000–1000 B.C.)

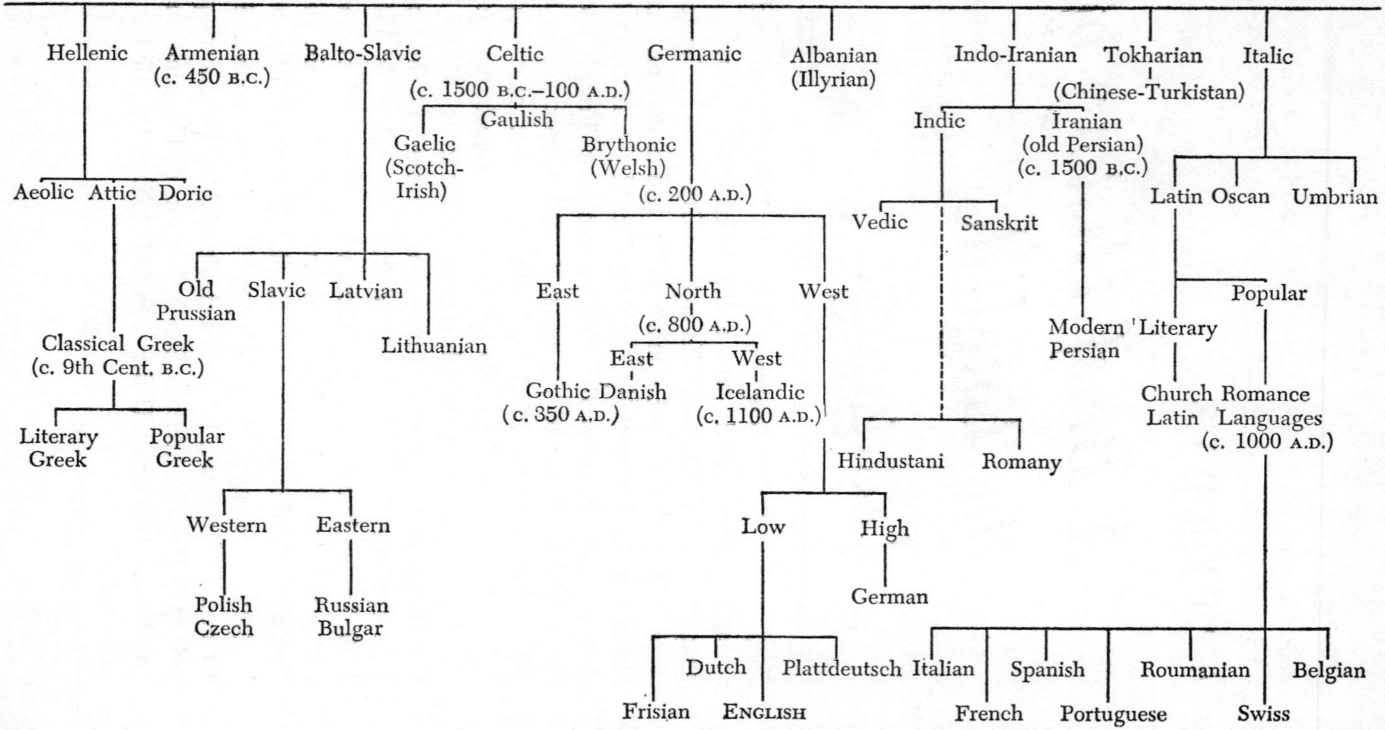

tinued to grow and develop in both structure and vocabulary in a relatively straight line leading utlimately to American English.

Anglo-Saxon was a completely inflected language; that is, as in Latin, word relationships tended to be expressed by word endings. As English evolved from its Germanic and Anglo-Saxon origins, it lost much of this inflected character. In modern English, function is expressed by word order not word endings. Prepositions have become vastly more important. Only the inflections for plural and possessive forms remain in use, and many of the irregular verbs still retain their ancient forms. The point always to remember is the fact that English word order is of the greatest importance in establishing meaning. In the sentence "The dog bites the man," we know that "dog" is in the nominative case and "man" is in the objective case because of their positions in the sentence. If we move "man" to the beginning of the sentence, then it will be in the nominative case, and the meaning of the sentence will be quite different.

Although words from other languages have been added to English throughout its history, in modern times it has almost been like a sponge–absorbing words into its vocabulary from every language with which it has come into contact. Many English words are of French origin (i.e., *reveille, colonel*), but many words also come from Italian (*piano*), from Spanish (*cañyon*), and even from Chinese (*chow*) and Japanese (*hibatchi*). A great deal of the English vocabulary, of course, has arisen as a result of a need for new terminology. For example, the word *broadcast,* thirty years ago, meant the spreading of seed by hand. The word was taken over by the radio industry, and its original meaning has nearly been lost. The creation of new materials has necessitated the coining of new words, usually from Latin and Greek sources (*nylon, rayon,* and *plasticon*). In some cases, new words, largely nouns, have been coined from people's names. For example, many of our streets are paved with a substance called *macadam.* This noun is derived from the name of the Scotsman who invented the substance, MacAdam. Much vocabulary also evolves out of slang. The word *butt,* meaning the end of a cigarette, was considered slang thirty years ago, but now it is a perfectly acceptable part of the formal language.

Modern American English is not terribly different from modern British English. It cannot really be considered a separate dialect. There are some differences in pronunciation, some differences in spelling (*harbor* in American English, and *harbour* in British English), and some differences in vocabulary (*petrol* in British English, and *gas* in American English). Basically, American English must be considered as a recent development of English—not a new or different language.

The exact future of the language, particularly of the American branch, is difficult to predict, but changes are going to continue as long as the language remains alive. In fact, today's speakers of English help to fashion it for future generations. Every person who coins a new word, a new idiom, a new expression may enrich our heritage. Every person who is satisfied with the cliché and the trite expression robs the language of its usefulness and its beauty.